CURRICULUM

Contemporary Art Goes to School

Edited by Jennie Guy

Bristol, UK / Chicago, USA

Editor: Jennie Guy
Assistant editor: Fiona Gannon
Copy-editor: Neil Burkey
Book design: Peter Maybury
Proofreader: Pamela Smith

Printed by Gomer
Paper: Munken Lynx and Munken Pure
Typefaces: Century Old Style and Foundry Monoline

Copyright © 2020 Jennie Guy
All rights reserved. No part of this publication may be reproduced, stored in a retrieval system or transmitted, in any form or by any means, electronic, mechanical, photocopying, recording or otherwise, without written permission.
A catalogue record for this book is available from the British Library.

Print ISBN: 978-1-78938-226-6

Art School gratefully acknowledges the financial support of the Arts Council of Ireland and the Arts Office of Wicklow County Council, Ireland.

www.artschool.ie

First published in the UK in 2020 by Intellect, The Mill, Parnall Road, Fishponds, Bristol, BS16 3JG, UK

First published in the USA in 2020 by Intellect, The University of Chicago Press, 1427 E. 60th Street, Chicago, IL 60637, USA

www.intellectbooks.com

Cover image: *Magnetic Fields*; Workshop series with artist Sven Anderson and Second through Fifth Year students; Scoil Chonglais, Baltinglass, Co. Wicklow; October 2015.

For my daughter
Molly Kay

CONTENTS

6   Foreword
             Gerard Byrne

14   Introduction
             Jennie Guy

32   *The Outline as Weapon*
             Nathan O'Donnell

42   *We Want to Learn How People Exist*
             Rowan Lear

52   *Image of the Self With and Amongst Others*
             Andrew Hunt

60   *In the Field*
             Helen Carey

70   *Weird Science*
             Hannah Jickling and Helen Reed

78   *The Masterplan*
             Juan Canela

86   *Dear Revolutionary Teacher…*
             Sofía Olascoaga and Priscila Fernandes

98   *A Suspended Focus: Art School 2014–2020*
             Jennie Guy, Peter Maybury, Fiona Gannon

212   *How Many Elsewheres? (For Four Voices)*
             Daniela Cascella

222   *38th EVA International: I Sing the Body Electric*
             Matt Packer

230   *Play Like Coyote*
             Alissa Kleist

240   *Exercising Study*
             Sjoerd Westbroek

252   *Art, the Body and Time Perspective(s) in the Classroom*
             Annemarie Ní Churreáin

262   *Preparatory Gestures for a Future Curriculum*
             Clare Butcher

274   Acknowledgements

Foreword
Gerard Byrne

CURRICULUM

> *It isn't necessary for a work to have a lot of things to look at, to compare, to analyze one by one, to contemplate. The thing as a whole, its quality as a whole, is what is interesting.*
> —Donald Judd, Specific Objects.[1]

As an adolescent my own thinking on art and education amounted to this: Art, the only thing I was interested in being good at, wasn't included in the school curriculum in my school, so art ≠ school. Clear. That hypothesis went fairly untested throughout most of my college education too. But now, as I read through this collection of texts I'm reminded of an occasion while I was an art student in New York in the mid-90s when I chanced my way into an opening at the old Metro Pictures Gallery on Greene St. in Soho. A complimentary beer successfully secured, I elbowed my way towards the art itself—a solo show of Mike Kelley. The show included the first ever exhibition of what would become a favourite work of Kelley's —*Educational Complex*.[2] The work is a large table-top architectural model combining every school the artist had attended, adjoined in a chronological order. This complex begins with his childhood home and ends with CalArts. The model, which Kelley's studio built solely based on his recollection, is in fact highly inaccurate. Somewhat ironically, I now see that this point of the model's inaccuracy has anxiously defined interpretations of the work ever since. Indeed, the dominant readings, which by informed accounts Kelley seems to have been amenable to, see the sprawling model as a sort of psycho-analytic analogue of what was remembered and what was 'effaced' or blocked out in Kelley's memory of his institutional education: an architectural map of trauma in absentia it would seem.

[1] Donald Judd, 'Specific Objects', in *Arts Yearbook* 8 (New York: The Art Digest 1965).
[2] *Educational Complex* (1995) was displayed as part of the exhibition *Toward a Utopian Art Complex* in the Metro Pictures Gallery, Soho, New York, from 21 October to 25 November 1995.

Foreword

For me that reading, intriguing though it is, instrumentalises the work in a literal way that undervalues some specific physical qualities of the work. *Educational Complex* isn't significant because it tracks Kelley's biography. Rather, its significance lies in its capacity as an artwork-cum-model to wilfully reconfigure relationships with educational institutions. Most interpretations agree the model is carceral in character, an amalgam of different institutions which have been conjoined in such a manner as to prevent the subject's escape. There are no gaps in this educational complex, whose form reminds me of a digestive tract. But *Educational Complex* is not actually a bona fide (i.e. accurate) model of something, nor is it a building. It is in fact a sculpture, and we as viewers are already positioned outside, and apart from it. We are liberated from the complex in question through our new roles as art viewers. The grace of Kelley's gesture in *Educational Complex*, which was made only months after his acclaimed Whitney museum show at the height of his career,[3] is his instrumentalisation of the moment of his canonisation to renegotiate his relationship with formal education through his own terms—through making a 'Mike Kelley' from all these troubling institutions. Like any art, in any gallery, anywhere, *Educational Complex* can be stood away from, interpreted, misinterpreted, laughed at, dwarfed and ultimately walked away from.

If after Yve-Alain Bois,[4] we see that to be an artwork is to already be a model for other artworks, we can see *Educational Complex* as one among many artworks as models for art and educational emancipation. In a different place, at a different time, Jennie Guy's Art School exceeds the rather stilted relations projected through *Educational Complex*, by calling upon a diverse set of progressive precedents from Artist Placement Group[5] to Paolo Freire[6] and Maria Montessori.[7] Guy's project relocates the emancipatory process to the school itself, and specifically public schools. As this publication evidences, the project that Guy has

---

3   *Catholic Tastes*, The Whitney Museum, New York, 1994.
4   Yve-Alain Bois, *Painting as Model* (Cambridge, MA: MIT Press, 1990).
5   The Artist Placement Group (APG) was an artist-led organisation initiated in the late 1960s by Barbara Steveni and John Latham. APG worked to emphasise the potential role of the artist in society, shifting the focus of artistic production from within the gallery and the museum to alternative sites such as within governmental, corporate and industrial infrastructures. Artists and movements who engaged with APG include

developed over recent years, is provocative in its low-key complexity. By purposely conflating and equating institutional languages of education to short-circuit certain institutional constraints, Guy signals her interest in engaging institutional education on a structural level. Just as the 'Art School' title conflates schools and art schools in a manner that provokes thinking around their differences, this book's title *Curriculum* is tested, challenged and often dismissed throughout the essays within. Nathan O'Donnell quotes John Baldessari on the untenability of art school curricula: 'There are no basic things. What's basic for one artist is not basic for another artist. And so you can't have basics; you can't build it in the normal curriculum way.'[8] Combining the standardised protocols and statutory regulations around public schools in all of their complexity with the highly individuated practices of established artists produces inherent contradictions. Negotiating these contradictions through delicate processes of identifying affinities and affirming commonalities for the diversity of stakeholders lies at the core of Guy's own work.

And yet Guy's practice is refreshingly comfortable in its own invisibility. Her labour is not displayed but is executed largely sotto voce. It's discreet, empathetic and aware. Through integrating, through negotiating, through the durability of relationships, and hard-earned judgement, and through an openness to risk, Art School is informed by the cumulative experience of each project but is focused on a different interest—change at an institutional level. As such, Guy's work engages its context in a different manner to that of most art, belying a practice that has equally been fed by her experience of parenting a child passing through the school system while witnessing the limitations of schools close up over an extended period. This dual insight of artist and parent underscores and informs much of what is in play throughout the project. For Guy's project involves openly testing the potential of combining both of these complex practices, school by school. Each situation is a

---

Joseph Beuys, Barry Flanagan, the Fluxus group and Yoko Ono.
6   Paolo Freire (1921–1997) was a radical educator focused on critical pedagogies, whose work emphasised learning as a collaborative exchange between student and teacher. Freire is the author of the foundational text *Pedagogy of the Oppressed* (1968).
7   Maria Montessori (1870–1952) was an influential educator whose innovative methods and focus on child-centred learning gave rise to an educational philosophy and system of schooling that bears her name.

controlled experiment, dispersing contemporary artists amongst groups of public-school kids and teachers, with lots at stake but little in the way of prescribed 'learning outcomes'. Convincing public schools to trust young people and artists' processes alike is not a given. As *Educational Complex* evidences, there isn't a deep well of trust to draw upon between contemporary art and public schools. Through staging this encounter between the two, Guy believes school kids are encouraged to renegotiate their relationships to (art-) school, allowing them scope to reposition themselves vis-à-vis the educational complexes to which they are tied. At the same time, Art School also provides progressive educators with unique arguments that can in turn feed into their future thinking.

The practices compiled in *Curriculum* are artistically diverse, but in drawing them together this book reveals a shared engagement in the historical legacies of progressive education through art. The material aggregated in these pages begins to reveal a sense of pattern, of tendency, of correspondence, which is largely obscured in the details of each project but which starts to shimmer rhythmically across the projects as a whole. These patterns are defined neither by shared aesthetics nor artistic ambitions. Rather, these patterns are circumstantial, perspectival, attitudinal and somewhat generational. Through gathering shared affinities and a common sense of the value of (re-)connecting public education with lessons learned through artistic practices, *Curriculum* provides a platform to finally see Guy's inconspicuously ambitious project Art School as a whole—a singular thing.

---

[8] Nathan O'Donnell's *The Outline as Weapon* can be read on page 32.

Introduction
Jennie Guy

Art School is a framework that brings established artists to work with students in both primary and secondary school settings through the organisation of workshops and artist-in-school residencies. I initiated the project in 2014 to explore the interfaces between schools and contemporary art by inviting students and artists to work collaboratively. This book, *Curriculum*, is a means of encountering Art School obliquely; texts intersect with projects along shoots and tendrils in a topical thicket formed around art and education. The texts contained within do not set out to accomplish the exhausting task of providing documentation and analysis of these projects. Instead, they work outwards to parallel each contributing writer's interests in these subjects, leaving Art School's timeline to be traced through a collection of annotated visual material, and the partnerships and affiliations that supported its evolution, detailed in the book's acknowledgements section. This introduction sets out the foundations on which Art School is based and still operates, particularly in this mode of reflection, and draws attention to the energy that it has generated.

    Although its scale is hard to define and its edges are uncertain, I will begin by attempting a quantitative summary. Since its inception, Art School has developed through fifteen projects conducted in Ireland. It has grown through the participation of thirty-three artists, over eight hundred students between the ages of six and eighteen, approximately seventy school teachers and staff, twenty primary and secondary schools, three third-level institutions, three national art centres, four county council arts offices and one national art biennial, and it has gained the support of a variety of regional and national arts and culture institutions in the process. I could go on in terms of videos made, tunnels drilled, strong men produced, gut bacteria cultured, mermaids dredged up and other aspects of the project's ecology, but I'll leave those ends loose, to be touched upon later on in this book.

In terms of its form, beyond the residencies and workshops at its core, Art School embraces mutation. It has grown to include exhibitions, publications, presentations, limited-edition posters and even an artist-led chat show. It develops by multiple stakeholders and agents conversing, proposing and negotiating, and is informed by each of its contexts, giving it a porous consistency, ready to mulch in and ferment on location.

Art School's energy is often provocative. Operating outside the constraints of the formal curriculum and enjoying freedom to experiment, the projects conducted under the aegis of Art School have addressed issues that are topical, pressing and often difficult to discuss. As students encounter artistic production through these subjects, they come to understand that art is much more than aesthetics, and can provide an opportunity to actively reassess a variety of concerns and find new ways of engaging with the world.

The time frames of projects vary considerably, as Art School does not adhere to a single format; workshops and residencies can take place over days in quick succession or extend across months. The day-to-day logistics of each project are negotiated on a case-by-case basis depending on the time and resources of both Art School and the school that is hosting it. Projects often begin with a site visit, where I have a chance to meet students, teachers, principals and other staff to work through the logistics and ambitions of the project across the table from each other. Following this, I often invite along the artist (or artists) to visit the school, so that they can be introduced to the students with whom they will work, plan their project, consider spaces they are curious to inhabit and enquire about other resources that they might be able to activate.

Given that Art School's modus operandi is constantly changing, writing proposals has always been an integral aspect of its adaptive architecture as an independent framework. Art School evolves through each proposal, via a new concept that responds to the specific context in which the project is to be set. These have included *Other? Other* Other!*, which explored otherness in the months following the Marriage Equality Act of 2015,[1] and *The Masterplan*, which investigated the changes occurring in Grangegorman, an area of Dublin undergoing rapid urban renewal.[2] Continually working to define the ambition of these projects has kept questions about the potential (perhaps occasionally elusive) role of art in relation to education close at hand.

Art has long had a place in school education, playing an important role in developing the skills, creative expression and imagination of students in the classroom. But the emphasis of art in the classroom setting often remains focused on cultivating a student's capacity to master established representational techniques and to develop a command over a particular medium. By contrast, Art School draws its inspiration from the active practices of contemporary artists who operate in a variety of media and engage with contemporary social, political and environmental issues such as climate change, urban regeneration, social dilemmas, protest, educational reform, abortion, teenage identity crises, migration, immigration and gender politics.

For example, during her residency at Killinarden Community School, artist Sarah Browne initiated an enquiry into knowledge transferal by showing students a hundred-year-old photograph of students learning to swim on dry land. This led to a discussion about how learning takes place—how it is mediated through mimicry, sensory experience, listening and demonstrating. The students then split into groups, each deciding on something they would like to learn and something to 'unlearn' (for example, the students voiced a desire to learn 'how people come up with

---

[1] Following a constitutional referendum in Ireland, the legal right for same-sex couples to marry was introduced in November 2015.
[2] Grangegorman is a new urban quarter being created in Dublin's north inner city.

ideas' and to unlearn 'how to use social media'). These aims were printed in poster format, and formed the beginning lines of a pantoum, which subsequently led to the development of a video work titled *How to Swim on Dry Land* that was exhibited in Rua Red as part of *It's Very New School* in 2017. In support of these sessions, Browne screened video documentation of other artists' work, including *Seven* by Mika Rottenberg and Jon Kessler.[3] This work involved participants being subjected to intense heat in a sauna-like container and pedalling exercise machines, wearing very little clothing, and producing sweat as the product of this labour. While this video was playing, I remember one of the students turning to me and asking, 'Are we allowed to be watching this?' This response made evident what was coming to mind for many of the other students, between scenes of skin, sweat and exertion. Screening this video in the classroom allowed space for thinking through associations between imagery, desire, objectification, competitive self-improvement and capital—an important and evocative knot to untangle in the context of this residency and beyond.

Processes like this might initially appear as unsettling within the context of education, as it is so often understood. Yet, inviting students, teachers and artists to open up and work on such subjects together through Art School has been an overwhelmingly affirmative experience. Perhaps this enthusiasm is a reflection of the challenging times in which we live and our growing sense that conventional modes of learning must adapt and change. Over the years that Art School has been active, it has operated against a backdrop of social, political, economic and environmental change which has manifested in both positive and negative ways in Ireland, as well as on a global scale: social reforms in Ireland, for instance, have extended the rights of women and LGBTQ+ people while, at the same time, a housing crisis has led to a catastrophic rise in homelessness;[4] and the climate crisis has sparked a surge of resistance

---

3 Mika Rottenberg and Jon Kessler presented *Seven*, a live artwork incorporating seven participants and a video installation, at the Nicole Klagsbrun Project Space in New York as part of *Performa 11*, 2011.

4 The Eighth Amendment to the Irish Constitution, giving an equal right to life to both the unborn and the mother, was repealed following a referendum held on 26 May 2018 allowing abortion services to be made available in Ireland. In terms of the homelessness crisis, it is not unusual for the children who have taken part in Art School projects to be

in defence of the interconnected nature of life on our planet, particularly among the young. Contemporary art offers a mode of interrogating these momentous changes, often in ways that are free from the constraints which become embedded within a formal curriculum. The support that Art School has received from arts organisations is also a sign of the growing recognition of the potential of art. There has been an expansion of interest in arts-in-education programming in Ireland, as evidenced by the Arts in Education Charter,[5] the National Arts in Education Portal,[6] modulating support structures within the Arts Council (Ireland's major arts funding body),[7] and, more recently, Creative Ireland.[8] Indeed, the initial stages of Art School were supported by the Wicklow County Arts Office's fledgling arts-in-education programme, Thinking Visual.[9] This interest in the role of art within educational reform extends into popular culture and media as well, with *The Sunday Times* devoting a full spread to the Art School exhibition *It's Very New School* in 2017.[10]

When introducing the Art School framework to an artist, I emphasise that the goal is to develop workshops and residencies where they can continue their own practice, based on their own research, their own working methodologies and their own beliefs. They do not have to 'perform' the role of the artist. Nor should they distil their practice into a format that can be easily evaluated or appraised in order to be legitimised within the school. In fact, the artists whom I have invited to work within Art School are not selected because of previous experience of working in schools. Instead, I approach each artist based on my interest in their current practice and recent exhibitions, sensing that the ways in which they work—or the themes that they explore—will resonate with students within a school setting. For the artist, whose projects and working practice constitute their professional identity, this process of shifting their interests towards the context of the school can be challenging. Nevertheless, the ongoing experience of Art School demonstrates that

---

living in temporary emergency accommodation.

5   The Arts in Education Charter was launched in 2012 as a collaborative initiative of the Department of Education and Skills (DES) and the Department of Arts, Heritage and the Gaeltacht (DAHG). For more information see education.ie, Publications, Policy Reports, Arts in Education Charter (PDF).

6   The Arts in Education Portal was launched in 2014, extending from the Arts in Education Charter and providing an online resource showcasing arts-in-education projects in

artists can occupy the space between the independence of their individual practices and the constraints that are embedded in the lived, experienced environment of a school.

The students' role (and experience) is crucial to the unfolding of each encounter. While they are invited into the unique world of each artist's practice, students are encouraged to become critically engaged co-producers. This means that artists and students might reciprocally influence each other in ways that have the potential to extend beyond the time they spend together. The nature of this co-production and the relationship between students and artists vary from project to project. Usually an open dynamic has been initiated through a specific moment which served as an icebreaker. I can recall a change in students' expressions when one of the artists informed them that they were terrible at drawing, and yet that they were artists as well! Or when another artist told the students that they really should go to visit IMMA (the Irish Museum of Modern Art) because, as the people of Ireland, they owned it. I remember a moment when a student's infant simulator cried out during a performance of John Cage's *4'33"*, its robotic cry followed by muffled laughter as we all tried to focus on the remaining period of 'silence'.[11] Or the look of astonishment and excitement on a group of students' faces when Maria McKinney described how she made a sculpture to be placed on an Aberdeen-Angus bull using more than 7,000 artificial insemination straws woven together like a corn dolly or a St Brigid's cross. Every project generated a moment in which the students' expectations shifted, and in which they realised that there was potential to develop something new, something unknown and not predetermined. The group dynamics during Art School sessions often surprised teachers who sat in to observe them, as quieter students often became actively involved, and different teams of students formed as they negotiated the new activities that they were working to accomplish together. As projects often shifted outside of

Ireland. To access the portal, see artsineducation.ie.

7 Creative Ireland is an integrated cultural programme launched in 2016, promoting participation in cultural activity on a variety of scales. For more information see creativeireland.gov.ie.

8 The Arts Council in partnership with the Department of Education and Skills and the Department of Culture, Heritage and the Gaeltacht launched the Creative Schools initiative in 2019, as a flagship initiative integrated in the Creative Ireland programme.

the classroom—incorporating corridors, gymnasiums, playing fields and other shared spaces—the students' sense of involvement and ownership grew even stronger, as they experienced what it felt like to perform these actions with the eyes of other students and school staff upon them.

The attitude of the hosting school is also decisive in the formation of each project. As places of learning charged with delivering knowledge and assessing understanding, schools have to be organised. Learning is to be quantified and measured, and there is considerable pressure to achieve year-on-year improvement. Creativity and innovation are sincerely declared as educational values, but they are difficult to instil—let alone to measure. Projects with indeterminate outcomes are therefore both an opportunity and a challenge. The teachers, special needs assistants, principals and school staff do much to set the atmospheres for these projects; they create the time and space for them to happen, and build a mood of anticipation. This is challenging, as there is no simple procedure for schools to open their doors to processes that are not laid down in the neatly tabulated curriculum and the routines of the academic calendar: Art School projects can spill outside the classroom and take root in different parts of the school; they might draw resources in terms of the time and attention of teachers and staff; and they might activate subjects and concepts that are not easily addressed.

Curriculum—this book—is a means of continuing to evolve the collaborative research and production supported by Art School between 2014 and 2020. In each essay, a different writer approaches a distinct aspect of Art School, whether a specific set of workshops, a single artist's work or a theme extrapolated from a cluster of projects. Along with these essays, the book includes a collection of annotated visual material which provides a glimpse of different Art School projects as they took place. Most of these images are stills taken from video that I captured while working with the artists in the schools; thus, they provide an active trace

---

For more information see artscouncil.ie, Arts in Ireland, Young People, Children & Education, Creative Schools.

9   The Thinking Visual programme initiated by arts officer Jenny Sherwin supported Art School residencies and workshops at multiple schools in Co. Wicklow between 2014 and 2018. For more information see wicklow.ie, Arts, Heritage & Archives, Arts, Programmes & Initiatives, Thinking Visual.

10 Cristín Leach, 'Lessons for Us All', *The Sunday Times*, 19 March 2017.

of the interaction between artists and students, as well as a sense of the school environments in which these projects took place.[12] The images also present several projects that do not feature explicitly in the essays, but that formed part of Art School nonetheless.[13] This intertwining of texts, images, projects, works, themes and authors reflects the collaborative working process of Art School itself.

The thirteen texts in *Curriculum* are as varied as the projects they discuss: some authors have responded in fiction or through dialogue, while others provide vivid contextualisation of the artists and projects. The brief given to the authors was not to document the projects in detail, but to approach them as points set along longer trajectories interweaving art, education and art education. In this way, specific encounters—actual exchanges in Irish schools—are opened up to both global and local considerations: some authors compare Art School projects to initiatives in other places (and other times), while other authors consider how these works resonate in the settings in which they were produced. Moreover, sharing the open-ended spirit of Art School itself, the authors were encouraged to approach the projects as active references rather than as finished products or as case studies that could be analysed and replicated. Considered together, these essays constitute a space of production in themselves—where new questions can emerge and resonate between writers and concepts, and where affinities among the insights gained through Art School can rise to the surface.

The book begins with Nathan O'Donnell's essay 'The Outline as Weapon'. O'Donnell directly confronts the unwieldy subject of art in education, discovering a means of contextualising Art School through a consideration of the artist's outline as a structural (and structuring) device. The essay reveals the outline to be both a fragile bureaucratic artefact as well as a powerful negotiating tool for establishing complicity, depending on how it is used. The text questions the disciplinary

---

[11] An infant simulator is an electric doll that teenagers are given in school to look after for a number of days. This is intended to give a sense of the responsibility of being a parent, though their efficacy in deterring pregnancy has been questioned.

[12] Many of the videos from which the still images used in this book were extracted can be viewed online at artschool.ie.

[13] Projects that appear in the visual material but do not feature in the essays include *Bead Game* (realised in collaboration with Fiona Hallinan) and the permanent artwork

prerequisites that are often mistakenly projected onto artists working in educational settings. Through this process, O'Donnell establishes a more nuanced perspective concerning the migration of instincts and resources that accompanies and supports this field of practice.

In 'We Want to Learn How People Exist', Rowan Lear delves into her own memories of school, bridging from recollections of the gymnasium ('I once lost a long swathe of skin to a gym hall floor') to a work developed by artist Sarah Browne in collaboration with students at Killinarden Community College. Retaining a focus on the architecture of the gym hall, Lear's contribution considers movement, bodies, collision, injury and collaboration. Lear treats Browne's video work *How to Swim on Dry Land* as a lens through which to observe the effects of order and disorder that contemporary art can have in educational settings.

Andrew Hunt's essay 'Image of the Self with and Amongst Others' echoes the title of Mark O'Kelly's residency with Transition Year students at Our Lady's School in Terenure, Co. Dublin.[14] The text highlights a series of paradoxes that emerge via a communally developed painting produced as this project's primary outcome. By exploring how the medium of painting is reactivated as it is integrated in social and community processes, Hunt draws attention to preconceptions concerning labour, the artist's studio and the commodification of art.

Helen Carey's text examines independent curatorial practice through the trope of 'the field', charting a relationship between less certain territories and more established institutions. The essay questions how the independent curator can reveal the kinds of lived knowledge that emerge within this tension, focusing on socially engaged practice and considering how to establish projects that activate both the independent and the institutional sides of this divide. 'In the Field' concludes with a brief encounter with *It's Very New School* (2017), an exhibition at Rua Red Arts Centre that covered four years of Art School projects.

Your Seedling Language (by Adam Gibney for St Catherine's National School in Rush, Co. Dublin).

[14] Transition Year is a one-year school programme that can be taken in the fourth year of secondary school in Ireland and in which multiple extracurricular subjects and projects are introduced to students. It is optional in most schools and compulsory in others, while in some schools it isn't feasible, and is skipped.

Hannah Jickling and Helen Reed's contribution, 'Weird Science', oscillates between the authors' own experiences working in schools in Canada and their engagement with Maria McKinney's workshop series *Birds of Prey*, developed with students at St Mary's National School in Maynooth. The authors characterise schools as a space of 'joy, subversion, control, kindness, chaos, bullying and friendship', and thus a productive environment for experimentation and intervention. Jickling and Reed chart McKinney's curiosity in developing artworks for (and with) animals, passing through considerations of genetics and breeding before linking back to issues of children's taste as explored in their own work *Big Rock Candy Mountain*.[15]

Juan Canela's contribution considers *The Masterplan*, a two-stage project featuring John Beattie and Ella de Búrca's work with primary school students in the Dublin 7 Educate Together National School, and Karl Burke and Naomi Sex's introduction of Transition Year students from St Paul's CBS Secondary School to the facilities and teaching in Dublin School of Creative Arts, TU Dublin. Embedded in a neighbourhood that is currently undergoing rapid redevelopment, the project speculates on how (and even if) individuals from different communities might become more aware of each other, looking particularly at the affinities between younger school students and the resources of a nearby university. Canela uses the project as a lens to scrutinise methods that might empower neighbours to explore the strengths that arise through proximity. The essay questions compliance and non-compliance, considering how local residents might have an active voice within the process of urban regeneration.

'Dear Revolutionary Teacher…' emerges from a dialogue between curator Sofía Olascoaga and artist Priscila Fernandes. Initiated via Fernandes' work *A friend in common*, commissioned for the Art School exhibition *It's Very New School* in 2017, the text delves into the history

---

15 *Big Rock Candy Mountain* is a public artwork by Hannah Jickling and Helen Reed sited in an East Vancouver elementary school, produced by Other Sights for Artists' Projects.

of Francisco Ferrer i Guàrdia's Modern School (Escuela Moderna), a primary school for children and their parents that existed between 1901 and 1909 in Barcelona. Linking back to Fernandes' ongoing research into this subject, the text invites the reader to reflect on the continued currency of Ferrer's ideas by reading a series of fictitious letters that the educationalist could have written and received from artists of the day, including Van Gogh and Matisse.

Daniela Cascella's 'How Many Elsewheres? (For Four Voices)' proposes a labyrinthine exploration of sound and listening as a new means of coming to know what it is to be in school. Cascella's four voices follow auditory traces that transform the potential of the classroom and the relationships that it seeks to contain, drawing inspiration from two series of workshops led by the artist Sven Anderson in Co. Wicklow. The text recalls the spatial deviations, divisions and cuts of Gordon Matta-Clark as it considers a semi-permanent outdoor sound installation developed by Anderson with Transition Year students in Blessington Community College, which prompted the exclamation: 'WE MADE A HOLE IN THE SCHOOL!'

Matt Packer writes about *I Sing the Body Electric*, a series of workshops developed in collaboration with curators Clare Breen, Orlaith Treacy and Maeve Mulrennan with students from three West Limerick National Schools as part of the 38th EVA International festival in 2018. This Art School project explored the possibility of integrating workshops focused on curatorial practice (as opposed to artistic practice) within a primary school setting. Packer considers how the project coincided with EVA's own historical approach to integrating educational initiatives, alongside education and outreach programmes developed by other art institutions and biennales abroad.

Alissa Kleist investigates the potentially subversive role of artists within sites of education, sensing their freedom to move beyond 'an exchange that ends in a form of closure' towards one of 'inconclusive interaction that does not necessarily seek resolution'. Kleist's text discovers a series of workshops led by artists Hannah Fitz, Jane Fogarty and Kevin Gaffney, with primary school students in Tisrara, Brideswell and Feevagh National Schools in Co. Roscommon. Kleist trains her focus on the prominent role played by animals within Gaffney's workshops and broader practice, discovering that the artist can literally 'Play Like Coyote', as the essay's title suggests.

Sjoerd Westbroek takes the writers' brief to its logical conclusion, positioning himself within the experiential framework explored in this book. 'Exercising Study' develops through Westbroek's engagement with a series of cues sent to him by artist Rhona Byrne, developed in an exchange related to Art School workshops led by Byrne with Transition Year secondary students in Blessington Community College in Co. Wicklow and primary school students in Gaelscoil de hÍde and Scoil Mhuire National Schools in Co. Roscommon. Branching off to intersect with workshops led by Elaine Leader with Transition Year secondary students in Blessington Community College, the text weaves these two artists' works around the experience and conditioning of physical space. The text probes the differences between learning and studying, thoughts that were triggered when accidentally overhearing a fellow train passenger declare 'I want to study, I do not want to learn' while rereading Stefano Harney and Fred Moten's book *The Undercommons*.

By drawing attention to the temporal dynamics of the classroom, Annemarie Ní Churreáin considers both the potential and the responsibility encountered by artists working in schools. 'Art, the Body and Time Perspective(s) in the Classroom' advances through Art School residencies and workshops developed by Vanessa Donoso López, Jane Fogarty, John Beattie and Ella de Búrca, considering how these artists approach time in their work with younger audiences. The essay draws from Lopez's work with primary school students in Gaelscoil de hÍde and Scoil Mhuire National Schools in Co. Roscommon, Fogarty's anthro-geological project with primary school students in Feevagh and Tisrara National Schools in Co. Roscommon, Beattie and de Búrca's compositional and performance studies with primary school students in the Dublin 7 Educate Together National School, and a collaborative production by Beattie, de Búrca and myself for the exhibition *It's Very New School* (2017) in Rua Red.[16] The essay integrates experiences gained through Ní Churreáin's practice as a poet working in schools, questioning the outsider's role in researching the mechanics of time as they influence education.

Curriculum draws to a close with Clare Butcher's 'Preparatory Gestures for a Future Curriculum'. Butcher's text contemplates an artist residency in Blessington Community College led by artist Sarah Pierce. Pierce's workshops evolved through an exploration of Bertolt Brecht's *Lehrstücke*, a form of experimental theatre that dissolves the boundaries between actors and audience to explore the revolutionary potential of the medium. Butcher's text engages with Pierce's instincts to embed a type of performative pedagogy within the group of students themselves, questioning whether it is possible to measure or evaluate a work of art that is registered in the bodies and the lived experience of those who were both its producers and its primary audience. The work converges on resolutions but not on a final product. Butcher's rumination on *The Square*—the central black square at the heart of Pierce's residency—serves as an apt parallel to the trajectory of Art School itself. Being situated in a mode of continuous rehearsal provides a powerful sense of freedom and agency.

I hope that this book's title—*Curriculum*—helps to ensure that it will find its way to a variety of readers who might encounter these essays as a means of seeing how contemporary art can be brought to a school

---

[16] This piece for the exhibition *It's Very New School* at Rua Red Arts Centre consisted of a sound installation and a floating shelf which held a series of custom-made books. The books' spines were imprinted with a selection of students' poetic answers to the questions 'What is school for?', 'What was school for?' and 'What will school be for?', creating an overlap between the universal and the individual, and reminding the spectator that any one question can have a universe of answers.

context in order to question the structures through which we choose to teach and to learn. To me, these essays suggest ideas that extend beyond the classroom—and outside of the realm of formal education—and towards different situations in which contemporary art can instigate change. As it builds through these texts, the curriculum that the book encounters (if indeed it does discover such a structure) is transitory, and always in flux. It emerges not from a universal enquiry, but through the specificity of individual practices that converged within real spaces, led by the instincts and interests of students who were only encountering these ways of working and thinking for the first time.

This book owes immense gratitude to all of the students, artists, teachers, principals, school staff and other supporters who contributed to Art School projects as they formed; to the writers and other contributors who have put so much energy into this book; and to the Arts Council of Ireland and the Arts Office of Wicklow County Council for generously funding this book's production.

The outline as weapon
Nathan O'Donnell

[i]

The 2009 MIT publication on art education, *Art School (Propositions for the Twenty-First Century)*, features—among a series of interviews, essays and architectural surveys—the transcript of a conversation between two artists who had been involved in teaching at important art schools during flourishing periods in the 1970s and 1980s: Michael Craig-Martin, who taught at Goldsmiths, and John Baldessari, who taught at CalArts. Their conversation hinges upon the question of what precisely makes such moments of flourish possible; what it is that makes an art school work.

Both seem to be in agreement that it is not about 'teaching', per se. Baldessari observes that in its early years there was no curriculum at CalArts. Instead they resort to discussions of atmosphere and relationship. They talk about creating a 'sympathetic ambience'. They admit this is a tentative formulation, but even the most successful art schools have highs and lows, cycles of success and inertia. Neither of them seem to be willing to endorse any kind of programmatic solution to the question. Instead, they claim, for an art school to function, it must simply assemble artists who are working actively and energetically in their own right and allow an environment to develop around them.

What Craig-Martin and Baldessari seem to be saying is that the sheer fact of an artist's proximity can have educational value—that the art school is more of a complex ecology than a logical system determined by ordinance and efficiency. This can be explained, at least in part, by the fact that contemporary artists' practices have no common universal basis, no grounding in a particular skill, say, no agreement on what Baldessari refers to as 'basic things':

Which is why you can't have a proper curriculum. There are no basic things. What's basic for one artist is not basic for another artist. And so you can't have basics; you can't build it in the normal curriculum way. The amazing thing about young people is they can jump in at a very sophisticated level without actually understanding what they're doing. Somehow that innocence allows them access to something. And so a part of teaching is helping them realize what it is that they've stumbled on.

Craig-Martin responds with the somewhat separate but nonetheless pertinent observation that '[a]rt schools are unlikely bedmates with universities… It's a very uneasy alliance.'[1]

Their conversation is enlightening, but there is little auto-criticism in evidence. Instead a tone of self-satisfied bemusement pervades the discussion—as if they're both just a bit baffled by the success of the schools they've been involved with. This is a performance, of course, but it is nonetheless striking that even those who have been key participants in what are acknowledged to be important institutions for art education have no real sense of what art education is—beyond the fact that it is not like other kinds of education. That it is in some way anti-systematic is agreed; this is a point that comes across in most commentaries on art education. Other than that, however, no one seems to know why art schools work. No one seems to know what art education actually is.

[ii]

When I got the invitation to contribute to this collection, I thought I would develop something about this idea of proximity. I didn't at all anticipate writing an essay about outlines.

---

1 John Baldessari and Michael Craig-Martin, 'Conversation', in *Art School: Propositions for the Twenty-First Century*, ed. Steven Henry Madoff (Cambridge, MA: MIT Press, 2013), 45. This book presents a number of 'propositions' by prominent art critics and theorists on the value of art education, alongside a set of 'profiles' of significant school buildings, an unusual conjunction of the theoretical and the concrete. This structure occasionally threatens to undermine the rich, provocative set of critical propositions arranged by

To clarify: when I talk about an outline here, I mean a class plan or schedule, a document laying out a teacher's or facilitator's intentions for a workshop or educational session. I have so many outlines on my laptop, spread across so many folders, it would be difficult for me to count them. I've been trained specifically in the preparation of outlines, as part of a teaching module I did in a university years ago. Most of us who work in an education environment—as teachers, artists, lecturers, facilitators—use outlines.

That said, outlines are rarely considered as anything other than functional documents. They serve a valuable purpose, but they are also strangely throwaway. To be honest, before the invitation to write this essay, I'd never given them a second thought.

[iii]

I have had several conversations with Jennie Guy over the past few years about Art School; it has been interesting to have this discussion against a backdrop of increasing receptivity, in Ireland at any rate, of the value of art in education. For example the Arts in Education Charter was signed in 2012, and the subsequent 'Portal' launched in 2015; likewise the educational imperatives of Creative Ireland (initiated in 2017, under one of its five 'pillars') represent another official formulation for administering certain kinds of creative pedagogy and engagement. Art School differs from such initiatives, however, in the way it configures the *exchange*. The priority of Art School has always been the protection of the artist's freedoms. Guy describes a working principle that is radical in its simplicity: the idea is to let artists practise, in their own way, within an educational setting.

What this entails is a refusal to participate in a system that sometimes sees artistic practice reduced to a supporting role, a means

editor Steven Henry Madoff, containing the radicalism of the book's more forthrightly anti-institutional contributors within the framework of already-extant building-based educational institutions and projects, however ambitious these may be.

of illustrating or serving some other pedagogical or curricular function. Such slippages are unfortunately common in a highly systematised formal education structure, particularly at secondary level.

This presents a number of challenges to a curatorial framework like Art School. Safeguarding the artist's autonomy requires ongoing vigilance and care on Guy's part. This is not to suggest that schools or educators are necessarily hostile to the artist; in fact, many of the schools who have engaged with Guy's project have been welcoming, enlightened environments for artists to work within. In a more general way, however, the methods of the contemporary artist can often appear alien to the educational landscape. It is part of the training of the artist, after all, to query the boundaries of what is and can be known, what is and can be taught. It is part of the training of the artist to query the *raison d'être* of 'school' as we understand it. So naturally there are moments of friction. In the case of Art School, these frictions have in some instances come to fuel the projects themselves. In Sarah Pierce's project, *The Square*, for instance, the strictures of the school timetable led to a very tight timeframe for the realisation of the project, which involved students generating a piece of collaboratively scripted theatre in response to a black square on the wall of the school gymnasium. In this case, the restrictions imbued the work with a sense of urgency and force.

As I see it (and I say this as someone who has taught, and continues to teach, in the disciplinary environment of the university), such moments of friction might be—at least in part—attributed to a mismatch in *disciplinarity*. Several theorists of art education make use of this term or some variant thereof in their speculations. Mick Wilson, for instance, describes the work of the contemporary artist as an 'undisciplined, adisciplinary, radically autonomous' field founded upon 'radical alterity'.[2] Similarly Charles Esche has described art education as anti-specialisation, anti-hierarchy and anti-autonomy.[3] This question of

---

2 Mick Wilson and Schelte van Ruiten, eds., *SHARE Handbook for Artistic Research Education* (Amsterdam: ELIA, 2013), 31.

3 Charles Esche, 'Include Me Out: Preparing Artists to Undo the Art World', in *Art School: Propositions for the Twenty-First Century*, ed. Steven Henry Madoff (Cambridge, MA: MIT Press, 2013), 101–13. There is an interesting disparity here between Wilson's proposition of 'radical autonomy' and Esche's quite distinct sense of the 'anti-

'discipline' is something I have looked at elsewhere in connection to the disciplinary structure of the university.[4] In that essay, I was interested in the relationship of contemporary art to the boundaries by which knowledge is organised. A related question is under scrutiny here however, i.e. the relationship between art and curriculum, the means, that is, by which such disciplinary knowledge is disseminated and reproduced. For, if contemporary artists work against discipline—against customary demarcations of knowledge—then the idea of the curriculum surely presents a problem. A curriculum is a way of systematising and imparting knowledge according to some agreed disciplinary boundaries: knowledge is classified according to subjects that come to seem like *a priori* divisions in the way the world is ordered—Geography, Physics, Classics, Maths. If we are to look at things sceptically—the way radical educationalists and theorists do—we could view school as an engine for the dissemination of this stratified world view, while an artist's job, or a certain kind of artist's job, or a part of a certain kind of artist's job, is to query such stratifications. Naturally there are going to be these moments of friction. In this respect, the outline becomes something like a buffer, a means of negotiating this hazardous exchange.

[iv]

Three years ago, long before I'd received the brief for this essay, I remember meeting Hannah Fitz at the side door of Temple Bar Gallery and Studios. Fitz had a studio there at that time. She was on her way back from a day-long session as part of an Art School project taking place at two schools in Roscommon (Brideswell and Feevagh National Schools), for which Fitz was one of three commissioned artists, alongside Jane Fogarty and Kevin Gaffney, working on drama and visual art exercises—creating short plays and tableaux vivants—with students.

---

autonomous' aspect of art education, but both are united in their sense that art education has to work against discipline, against specialisation.

4 Nathan O'Donnell, 'Complementary Studies', *Paper Visual Art Journal* 8 (Winter 2017): 13–26.

She was stepping in as I was stepping out the side door of the studio complex. She was carting boxes of materials. I wedged the door open and helped her lug things inside. She was, she told me, exhausted. It's funny, she said. We are just there to make work, that's the brief, to go and practise as we normally would, as artists, but in a school. You'd think that would be straightforward, she said, but I am absolutely wrecked. She didn't mean that as a negative thing. She was just surprised, I think, at having been able to spend a whole day, with a group of children, simply *making*.

[v]

An artist's outline is not the same thing as a teacher's outline, of course. Teachers—and this seems to me the fundamental difference—work within a curriculum. They have a body of knowledge or a set of imperatives that it is their job to impart or enact. I have worked as an artist-in-residence at a school where it was hoped that I might engage with the curriculum, and I guess this is probably not unusual, but it is certainly not a hugely useful way to engage an artist in a classroom.

As the plan for this essay developed, I asked Guy to send me along some sample outlines. Viewing them together I was struck by their sheer variety. Some artists stay very close to the facts, listing simply the physical actions and exercises they will carry out. Others embrace the language of methodology and objective, finding ways to link their ideas with the familiar structures of the classroom, quantifying the educational benefits of their work, 'problem-solving', 'collaborative learning', 'lateral thinking'. (Some artists find this kind of structure helpful; others—I must count myself among the others—less so.) They are, in either case, rigorous and carefully constructed documents. The outline, whatever shape it takes, is an imperative part of the process.

[vi]

It seems to me you could look at the outline as the trace of a specific exchange between an individual educator (or in this case an artist) and an educational system. Every outline is the mark of a single interface between the particular and the general.

Of course the outline doesn't necessarily correlate to the reality of what took place in the classroom or workshop. It's not a record in that sense, or rather it's a record of a set of aspirations, or actually—in many cases—not even aspirations, but defences against contingency. It is a way of buttressing against disorder. It is in some senses a weapon.

[vii]

I met with Guy and Sven Anderson on a bright evening at Anderson's studio, to talk about this essay and about the project overall. The sun was going down over the eighteenth-century square outside.

We talked again about the premise of Art School. It has always been an artist-centred programme, Guy said. The idea is not that the artist serves the school in some way, but that on the contrary the school becomes a site of artistic production. This is the project's fundamental premise.

Art School has always been a lean operation. Reliant upon occasional funding through whatever systems are in place—Arts Council, Per Cent for Art, local authority funding, departmental funding—there has never been scope for it to acquire the authority of an institution. Nor has that ever been an intention of Guy's. She has not set out to propose a solution to a problem. She is cognisant of several problems, of course, with the ways in which art is taught and viewed and (more recently) instrumentalised within Irish educational circles. But Art School has never aspired to fix these problems. Its remit has been more modest and more important, ultimately: to explore how artists might operate in a school setting, and to create a space for artists to experiment in this context.

We talked a bit about this, about how artists are trained to think in critical material terms about the world, about how things are made and why, about how to question their surroundings: vital things for young people to learn.

We talked about Guy's curatorial approach. It is, in part, she says, about generating protective mechanisms, allowing the artist to do what they do. There are always frictions. There are pressures to give answers at the outset, to tell the school or certain parties within a school what it is that the artist is going to do, when in fact artists don't work like that, beginning with an answer, formal or otherwise. The task is creating a space for uncertainty in an environment in which uncertainty is generally unwelcome. Even within the most welcoming schools, there is a delicate balance to be struck.

In a way, the real challenge is to allow for provisionality. Surveying those forms of art education (and other kinds of education) to which I've been attracted over the years, this allowance (for the makeshift, the contingent, the unexpected) strikes me as one notable common feature. Educationally innovative organisations—such as Edward O'Neill's Prestolee School in Lancashire, Francisco Ferrer's Escuela Moderna in Barcelona, A.S. Neil's Summerhill in Suffolk, or (somewhat later) the Scotland Road Free School established in Liverpool in 1966—provide historical precedent for a lineage of scattered educational initiatives.[5] Meanwhile, art schools following the example of institutions like Black Mountain College (those intentionally anti-systematic regimes described by Baldessari and Craig-Martin) became sites for non-disciplinarised, radically provisional learning.[6] The work of educational theorist Colin

---

5   On Prestolee, see Catherine Burke, '"The school without tears": E.F. O'Neill of Prestolee', *History of Education: Journal of the History of Education Society* 34, no. 3 (2005): 263–75. On the Escuela Moderna, see Geoffrey C. Fidler, 'The Escuela Moderna Movement of Francisco Ferrer: "Por la Verdad y la Justicia"', *History of Education Quarterly* 25, no. 1/2 (Spring–Summer 1985): 103–32. On Summerhill, see A.S. Neil, *Summerhill: A Radical Approach to Child-Rearing* (New York: Harold Hart, 1960). For further information on the Scotland Road School and other anarchist educational

Ward (aligned with a network of educational innovators in the 1970s that included Ivan Illich and Everett Reimer) is significant here too; in *Streetwork: The Exploding School*, he devised a proposition for a decentralised anarchist-inflected programme of devolved education that makes use of children's environments as instruments of learning.[7] One thing that unites these various educational programmes and propositions is the way they make use of their surroundings and the inherent relationships therein, allowing learning opportunities to emerge out of existing conditions rather than imposing upon them some set of pedagogical rules.

[viii]

I have shared outlines with other writers, artists, educators. I have had outlines shared with me. I have cut and pasted parts of other people's outlines, or used their headers, or selectively appropriated their terminology. Sentences have been patched together from several other people's outlines, themselves presumably cobbled together in much the same way. In terms of their genesis, outlines are hybrid monstrosities. They are part of an ecology of resource-sharing among those who work in educational environments, the outcomes of a complex genealogy of contingencies: scraps of technocratic language; hurried cut-and-pasting; pieces of strategic bad faith; as well as the sudden unlocking of connections; the sharing of ideas; the unexpected fruit.

---

projects in Liverpool, see an article originally published in *The Blast*, and republished on the radical resource-sharing website, libcom.org.

6 See Vincent Katz, *Black Mountain College: Experiment in Art* (Cambridge, MA: MIT Press, 2013). To trace the influence of the principles of Black Mountain College and the Bauhaus on British art education, see Nigel Llewellyn, *The London Art Schools: Reforming the Art World, 1960 to Now* (London: Tate, 2015).

7 See Anthony Fyson and Colin Ward, *Streetwork: The Exploding School* (London: Routledge and Kegan Paul, 1973).

We want to learn how people exist

Rowan Lear

I once lost a long swathe of skin to a gym hall floor. I don't remember falling, only running, tripping and then gliding through the air with serene grace, watching the lacquered surface skim past my outstretched arms. Eventually the journey was interrupted by that first, dull impact, but my velocity was such that I slid unstopping for a half-second or so, on the blunt end of one knee.

La–cer–a–tion—the word alone is a scream of mangled flesh. Now, the pain: the piercing of perforated epidermis. I gazed paralysed at my classmates, who were safely corralled at the far end of the hall, and at the teacher, who pointed to the benches at the side and proclaimed sternly: 'Out'. Jaw clenched—*do not cry, do not cry*—nothing makes one more insensitive than words.[1] I stood, refusing all injury, as if the body that had fallen to earth belonged to someone else.

It wasn't until reaching the shelter of a classroom desk hours later that I gingerly peeled back my tracksuit pants, curdled with something dark and oozing. Again as if from a great distance, I gazed at this abject and alien fascia. The wound resembled less flesh than the opencast coal mine located not so far from my school: a raw and bloody geology exposed to the sky—layers of excavation, pools of gathering fluid, and reams of dark matter that twist and turn and break and fault. Every mine is a line of flight.[2]

In that same classroom, I vividly remember being patched up by a teacher who distracted my tears with a lesson on the scab: its function as a physical barrier and a restorer of the skin's integrity, and the fact that the surface that grew back would never be precisely the same as before, never quite as seamless, never quite as smooth. The incident in the gym hall taught me something of pain and fear and shame and

---

1   Michel Serres recounts being stung by a hornet in the middle of a lecture, and continuing, because 'the speaking body, flesh filled with language, has little difficulty in remaining focused on speech, whatever happens' (Michel Serres, *The Five Senses* (London: Bloomsbury, 2009), 59). Words leave the body behind.
2   For Deleuze and Guattari, 'mines are a source of flow, mixture, and escape with few equivalents in history'. Even when ruled and managed by empires, mines and metals are the origin of unforeseen movement, insurrection and revolt among metallurgical

falling and healing and scarring—those most enduring lessons of twelve years of schooling. But it is the waxed, gleaming surface of the gym floor that lingers in my mind—the bland beige veneer, an interweaving mesh of yellow and white court markings, and that seductive, treacherous smoothness.

It was this memory that slid through the seams of my psyche, on a first viewing of *How to Swim on Dry Land*, a two-channel video work created by artist Sarah Browne and a group of pupils at Killinarden Community School, instigated as part of the project Art School. Though I watched it while stationary, in the habitual hunch of the laptop user, something of my body yearned to move. In an alternating half of the bisected screen, the camera skims the flat surface of a green laminated floor, following a singular court marking as it intersects and overlaps with others. We endlessly skate, curve, glide and turn sharply in pursuit, but never lose sight of the line.

The first Greek *gymnasia* were multidimensional: host to philosophical and intellectual discourse, as well as athletic activities. But these gyms were vast outdoor spaces, open to the sky. Their enclosure—becoming *hall*—is a much more recent endeavour. Despite multiple waves of outdoor leisure and open-air fitness movements in the nineteenth and twentieth centuries, the bulk of physical culture became gradually and immutably enclosed in the hall.

The enclosure of the gymnasium was, in the words of historian Henning Eichberg, 'part of a new pattern of relationships between the body and its environment'.[3] It concurred with other changes: natural obstacles like trees replaced by man-made equipment; the athlete freed from restrictive clothing but banished from the experience of weather; exercises practised haphazardly were formalised, militarised and performed by rank and file at command or timed intervals. And the spaces themselves were homogenised: progressively sealed from the

---

peoples and those with whom they trade and mingle.

[3] Eichberg is alert to bodies as active carriers of knowledge and the ways that bodily movement is increasingly calibrated by homogenous and restrictive architectures, technologies and techniques (Henning Eichberg, *Body Cultures: Essays on Sport, Space, and Identity* (London: Routledge, 1998), 55).

outside world, frequently windowless, air-conditioned and lined with sleek surfaces.

The architecture of the gym hall is no more or less natural than the crumbling sandstone façade of one school, the pitted concrete topography of another, or the smooth varnish of a desk, hewn by protractors and concealing a secret, sticky tundra of gum. These landscapes give rise to the very possibility of movement or stillness, of being contorted or standing tall. As Sara Ahmed writes, 'perhaps education is a straightening of what is already bent'.[4] Ironically then, my body is contoured by classroom furniture and its office successors: upper back in permanent disarray; fingers crooked from clutching pencils. The learning environment is neither indifferent nor uninvolved in shaping the bodies that collide with its edges.

At my school—and I expect, most schools—the gym hall was a smooth space striated by a multiplicity of activities. It was the site of exercise classes and ball games, but also assemblies, recitals, performances, detentions, workshops, rehearsals, dances and school dinners. Each demanded a different comportment, its own slippery set of standard operating procedures. Multifunctionality requires of the gym hall more than one kind of smoothness: it has to operate as physical *tabula rasa*, with flat mats and stackable benches. But it also carries a veneer of neutrality—bland, efficient and flexible—that conceals its disciplinary character.

It's quite different to the playground, whatever form that takes. Ours was a stretch of coarse, damp tarmac interrupted by patches of tangled weeds, nettles and sticky willy, tugging urgently at ankles and sleeves. Here, a potent politics is played out at an accelerated pace: alliances are formed, conflicts are triggered, riots unleashed, a chase is underway—a game of love and war that pauses only for the bell and the classroom intermission.

---

4 Ahmed describes the regulation of the child's will as a 'straightening device', and writes: 'If we have this understanding of will, we would not be surprised by its queer potential: after all, you only straighten what is already bent' (Sara Ahmed, *Willful Subjects* (Durham: Duke University Press, 2014), 7; 21).

The playground is wholly wild—'a wild place which continually produces its own unregulated wildness'—savage with the screams, cackles and wails of juvenescence.[5] Today, on approaching or passing a school during breaktime, something of the clamour incites a shudder, an innate terror, because the playground is perhaps a space—the only space—that truly belongs to children, and children alone. The adult is a trespasser, the territory now alien, the body grown no longer fits in its crevices.

Unlike the playground, the gym hall is not the site of open rebellion, nor the laboured and orderly learning of the classroom: spaces diametrically opposed in their function and effect. Rather, it is an interstice between the school and the outside: where vitality is captured, where frenetic is channelled into energetic. Its lessons are more insidious, because there is pain but also pleasure entangled in learning the ropes.[6] I recall the perverse joy earned by prevailing in the 'bleep test', a fitness exercise that compels runners to incrementally speed to a sprint between two points. Like the shuttle run or the squash game, the bleep test is compressed between arbitrary points in limited space. The gym hall—criss-crossed by court markings—is where we are literally taught to *toe the line*.

But, as my injured knee attests, bodies moving rapidly in close proximity in a compact space are a recipe for accidental collision. The concourse (*a running together*) and the discourse (*running back and forth*) of the gym hall are at odds with the curriculum (*race without deviation*) of the classroom, with its singular trajectory and endpoint.[7] Here, it is not merely possible but inevitable to swerve, diverge, get side-tracked and crash into one another.

Browne worked with students in their 'Transition Year', which is itself a moment of divergence from standard curricula, seemingly unique to Ireland's education system.[8] For a group of these students,

---

5   Jack Halberstam introduces Fred Moten and Stefano Harney's book *The Undercommons: Fugitive Planning and Black Study*—which advocates subversive intellectual practice in and against the institution—as 'a wild beyond to the structures we inhabit and that inhabit us' (Stefano Harney and Fred Moten, *The Undercommons: Fugitive Planning and Black Study* (Brooklyn, NY: Minor Compositions/Autonomedia, 2013), 7).

6   Felix Guattari recognises the 'family-nursery-school complex' as a conduit for libidinal

Browne devised a series of playful workshops, introducing a range of materials and approaches to contemporary art practice as cultural critique. These included artist instructional films, such as Martha Rosler's 1975 deadpan parody *Semiotics of the Kitchen* and Jillian Mayer's 2013 straight-faced satire *Makeup Tutorial—How To Hide From Cameras*, as well as historic photographs of blind children studying taxidermied animals through touch and classes in swimming taught on dry land.

In the latter images, from which the project draws its title, the bodies of children and young soldiers are poised horizontally over crates, benches and, most amusingly, their classmates, leaving arms and legs unencumbered to practise their strokes at the command of an instructor. It was the absurdity of swimming technique that inspired the anthropologist Marcel Mauss to write his classic essay 'Les techniques du corps' in 1934. He observed that the way he was taught to swim—whereby swimmers spat out water and 'thought of themselves as a kind of steamboat'—had disappeared within a generation, replaced by a completely new style. He determined that, in fact, there was no 'natural way' for an adult to move. From running and eating to sitting and sleeping, all habitual movements of the body are cultural techniques, composing 'physio-psycho-sociological assemblages' specific to the social and technological environment in which they are learned.[9]

This doesn't mean, however, that what is learned might be simply unfastened and rewired: Mauss struggles to rid his mind and musculature of his original swimming technique. He observes too that, during the war, no retraining could enable English and French infantrymen to march their mismatched gaits to the same tune, or even dig with each other's spades. Finally, Mauss notes that cultural techniques are not necessarily transmitted in a straightforward fashion, in the manner of a national directive. Assembled by and for social authority—even that of a collective

---

desire and a hotbed of 'micro-fascist seductions'. The *jouissance* of school life does not stem from any small freedoms that might be wrested from the educational machine: it is precisely connected to its repression of students' behaviour—the scheduling of work, the organisation of space, the restraint of movement and voice, and prohibition of corporeal and creative expression (Felix Guattari, *Schizoanalytic Cartographies* (London: Bloomsbury, 2013), 42–4).

7 Stephen Connor notes the preference for the concourse in Michel Serres' writing, who

or classroom—they are predominately passed down, through and across a social milieu, by imitation.

School is a stealth training camp, a 'civilising process', where mimicry reigns.[10] Gestures make gestures, postures produce postures, in a form of tacit study. Our bodies are wandering archives of that which we learned from other bodies. If there is a critical question at the core of *How to Swim on Dry Land*, it might go something like this: what did we learn when we were playing or not paying attention? And might those things be unlearned—or learned differently?

The second channel of *How to Swim on Dry Land*—forming a counterpart to the perpetual sweep over the gym hall floor—records various props as they come to be known by curious limbs: stroked, prodded, kicked, frayed, thrown and tapped. A patterned grey pebble is tumbled between hands, clasped to score a squiggly chalk line and booted gently across green linoleum. Sheets of card are torn and rolled and rasped against each other; glittering fingernails tap-tap-tap the seductive black mirror of a smartphone screen. There's a fist bump, a knock on a sky-blue wall, a door pushed open to blinding daylight. And a school bag adorned by pink and purple nebulas; a foil blanket crinkled, wrapped and hurled into space.

> What do we mean by art? It's not all about paint? When everyone was poor?… Boredom, to lift depression, to break silence, talent, express feelings… We want to learn about musical instruments… We want to unlearn social media… Snapchat, Facebook, Twitter… We don't do anything unexpectedly any more?… We want to learn how people exist… How was space created? Was the sea formed?… Sunsets are different on other planets… Will there be different art in the future? For different creatures?… We want to learn how people exist.

revels in 'the unpredictable rhythm of loops, leaps, poolings, spurts and recurrences' (Serres, *The Five Senses*, 1).

8   Devised to produce a pause in the academic structure, Transition Year offers students aged 15–16 forms of self-directed, vocational and life skills training, including group retreats, work experience and trips. In Ireland, Transition Year receives both praise and criticism, all of which adopts a neoliberal tone: either a doss year and a waste of time or fostering entrepreneurialism.

9   Marcel Mauss, 'Techniques of the body', *Economy and Society* 2, no. 1 (1973): 70–88.

The voiceover, in which different students read aloud poetic queries, recounts a list of things they desire to learn or unlearn. The tone here is not the ironic insincerity exemplified by some of the video works shown to the group; rather, it tends towards a kind of earnest but playful probing. The questions are at once mundane and profound, assured and uncertain—the kinds of questions I remember teachers ignoring, because they have no satisfying answers, only more questions. The repetition of the pantoum form, in which certain lines recur in new contexts, creates a circular structure—a running-together-back-and-forth—and a mesmeric refusal to conclude or settle on a final demand.

My school days were regularly enlivened by a friend who refused to settle. On the days that he forgot his pills, he would throw tables, build chair tunnels, abandon class and roly poly down the corridors, whooping as he passed open doors. He wasn't a clown (though we treated him as such) and he didn't crave attention (as teachers suspected). Nor was he incapable of sitting still: he simply had a singularly irrepressible desire to move, in a world incompatible with movement.[11]

While the rest of us scratched our lines of flight into desk graffiti, blew them in cigarette rings or carved them into skin, he refused such containment. Sometimes he ran for the school gates, but more often he stayed in the building, circumnavigating the corridors, darting into classes, evading the clutches of senior staff until the end of the day. Like the gym hall, the corridor is another interstitial space, another course for collision, another chink in the armour.

Today, artists are most often found in schools under official invitation.[12] They walk with shoulders weighted by certain expectations (of commissioners, teachers, students) as well as their own memories of education. A decade ago, on first finding myself back in a classroom wearing the Visiting Artist's badge, I naïvely imagined that what was at stake was the rewriting of the curriculum. How could a programme of

---

10 In a famous study, *The Civilising Process*, sociologist Norbert Elias traced the written and unwritten rules of behaviour and refinement of manners across Europe from the medieval period to the twentieth century, connecting individual discipline to changes in social organisation and state formation.

11 For Deleuze, a 'school' is the opposite of a movement. See Gilles Deleuze, Charles J. Stivale and Claire Parnet, *Gilles Deleuze from A to Z* (Cambridge, MA: MIT Press, 2011).

12 My only physical access to the microcosm of the school—after leaving at sixteen—has

study be changed, reoriented, extended and supplemented? How might an artist feed this project of expansion and enrichment?

It isn't uncommon for artist interventions to be captured wholesale for curriculum development, or used to improve students' university or career prospects.[13] Though these may be incidental outcomes of the project that placed Browne in the classroom, there is another, more urgent drive at its core. The parting shot of *How to Swim on Dry Land* is the opening of an inconspicuous doorway and an escape from the gym hall into daylight. It is a reminder that the walls of the classroom are never so solid that they cannot be breached by the very bodies they were built to contain. As with Fred Moten's description of the state, institutions of learning are more fragile, even aerated, than they first appear: 'There are all kinds of little holes and tunnels and ditches and highways and byways through the state that are being produced and maintained constantly by the people who are also at the same time doing this labour that ends in the production of the state.'[14]

When we artists enter the school, we might be receptive not only to our complicity with the education-industrial-complex, but to those gaps that are already present, and the kinds of learning that are already under way. Because, 'when we enter a classroom and we refuse to call it to order, we are allowing study to continue, dissonant study perhaps, disorganized study, but study that precedes our call and will continue after we have left the room'.[15] Wherever bodies are subject to training and the embedding of habits, there are unruly ruptures, acts of wilfulness and accidents that might also undo those habits. And sometimes these cracks open into the tunnels that lead elsewhere.

---

been as an invited speaker at 'creative industries' events designed to teach children about the worlds of work and higher education, or as an artist-in-residence, as part of an access to arts education programme run in collaboration with local art colleges. In both cases, the content and structure of my visits were planned, vetted and evaluated meticulously by a number of stakeholders (but not the students).

13 The artist collective Precarious Workers Brigade have organised precisely against this instrumentalisation of creative labour, writing: 'We don't want to reproduce a culture that generates neoliberal subjects, but rather we aim to encourage students

to become selves who can also act, resist and create alternatives' (Precarious Workers Brigade, and Silvia Federici. *Training for Exploitation? Politicising Employability and Reclaiming Education* (London: The Journal of Aesthetics & Protest Press, 2017), 9).
14 Fred Moten, in conversation with Stefano Harney and Stevphen Shukaitis (Harney and Moten, *The Undercommons*, 145).
15 Halberstam in Harney and Moten (Harney and Moten, *The Undercommons*, 9).

Image of the self with and amongst others

Andrew Hunt

I pick up the phone.
'Andrew?' a familiar voice says.
'Yes?'
'It's Mark O'Kelly, how are you?'

I tell Mark that I'm well and that I've been looking forward to speaking with him, especially about his residency that resulted in his large collaborative work *Image of the Self With and Amongst Others*. This painting was shown at the exhibition *It's Very New School* at Rua Red in Dublin, and alongside its connection to current discourses on the expanded field of painting,[1] it also connects to issues of gender and gesture, and holds a special relationship with the wider field of secondary education. Working with Transition Year students in Our Lady's School, Terenure, Mark produced a group portrait that spoke of his own desire to collapse social and cultural boundaries and his collaborators' wish to present themselves as they imagine they exist in their own community. In essence, this created a form of contemporary painting that problematises the role of the artist as educator within a non-hierarchical network of contributors both young and old, yet also forms a synthesis of both, including categories of lay audience and specialist elite.

During our conversation, Mark convinces me that he has a strong belief in the fact that there is no opposition between children's art and high theory, the university and the studio, or Fine Art from within the academy and that from outside. There's no war between the two poles designated by the oft-asked question, 'Do you get time between teaching to make your own work?' He also intelligently connects criticism with empathy and warmth to fuse a gap between forms of instrumental social populism and

---

[1] See for example writing by Isabelle Graw, Kerstin Stakemeier and David Joselit, on vitalism, 'networked painting' and philosophy over criticism conservatism, among many other subjects.

aesthetic liberation that is sometimes missing in much socially engaged art. In this respect, *Image of the Self With and Amongst Others* starts to exist as a humorous fusion of conflicting subjects, perhaps a riff on the bizarre plot of Terry Zwigoff's comedy-drama film *Art School Confidential* (2016), starring John Malkovich, Anjelica Huston, Sophia Myles and Max Minghella: Mark's engagement with the school creates a group self-portrait, made by the students, that produces a powerful transaction of performance-based painting that satirises singular masculine authority and sovereignty in a Wittgensteinian duck/rabbit process of ambiguity that asks the question, 'Who has the power: myself, the students, the institution or the intersection of all three in the aesthetic dimension of the work?'

The subject of this painting is therefore how an all-girl school can be choreographed by a middle-aged man in a self-consciously patriarchal relationship that links to art historical patronage, in a paradoxical attempt to level this very hierarchy through action and reflection, through graphology and gesture in a coherent manner. Furthermore, the work represents an attempt to generate new forms of self-consciousness around gender and painting—Mark is somehow self-consciously self-conscious about being self-conscious—in an ongoing process of feminist discourse that reveals ongoing power relationships by folding them back into painting in an encoded manner. As Joanne Laws has put it in relation to Mark's work in education, this mural serves to 'create counter-cultures to the so-called "factory model" of nineteenth-century education',[2] new institutional-critical positions that divulge hidden power dynamics.

If this performative dance around collaboration also uncovers saccharine and often naïve modes of political art practice that masquerade as portals to diversity, but which more often than not contain more than a faint whiff of puritanism (direct forms of political art that lack the aesthetic dimension necessary to allow a real shift to a disinterested

---

2   Joanne Laws, 'A lived activity, not an abstract pastime', catalogue, *It's Very New School*, curated by Jennie Guy, Rua Red Gallery, 2017.

meta-politics, so to speak), then this work operates satirically through the always-nearly-but-not-quite-redundant medium of paint. Painting is represented as an analogue dinosaur, impossibly situated in relation to a 'real' political art, within our technologically saturated present, yet paradoxically with transformative possibilities. Mark uses this to provocatively reference the earliest history of painting in human societies in a key reversal of views on contemporary technology and mark-making. Importantly, what's evident in the marks that the students have made is the historical origin of face painting, a form that pre-dates cave painting, a fact that Mark acknowledges in our conversation. This is a primal mode of identification that pole-vaults over long-historical time into the present as we approach the 2020s, in which selfies and identity politics dictate our existence in digital form. If group portraiture and the uses of the traditional family album have declined in favour of individual self-taken portraits circulated online, then this work exists as a multitemporal, multidimensional, multiauthored painting. Alongside this, *Image of the Self With and Amongst Others* supports a slow, durational-temporal resistance to the narcissism of social media and its increased pressure upon the psyche, which often promotes 'singular' notions of identity.

Mark says in our conversation that, in his view, in recent cultural history connected to the image of the face: 'If the 1960s were about lips (Mick Jagger and the Rolling Stones), and the 1970s were about eyes (David Bowie), then we can fast forward to 2019, which is all about Kim Kardashian and "eyebrows".' Here issues of body politics connect to young women's shifting identities, again in an intersectionality of community painting connected to digital communication. This work's reference to face painting isn't a riff on likeness, but instead connects to posture and attitude in the cultural force of celebrities such as Kardashian—the American media personality, businesswoman, socialite, model and actress—as well as to recent painting in the US, in the form of identity politics in a post-identity climate. This theme is also inherent in the work of Nicole Eisenman, which often toys with themes of sexuality, comedy and caricature.

One could claim that there is also a connection between other forms of diametrically opposed forms of painting, such as that represented by Amy Sillman's and Laura Owens' deliberately skewed lyrical abstraction on the one side, and Wade Guyton's cool digital printed paintings on the other. If, as mentioned above, theorists such as Benjamin Buchloh, Isabelle Graw and Kerstin Stakemeier have claimed that male lyrical abstraction, from De Kooning to Albert Oehlen, represents a slick lack of risk masquerading as experimentation, improv, immediacy and painterly mastery, then the opposite is true of Mark's painting with his young female students. As Mark says in relation to the planning of this work:

> Some great artworks are by their nature apparently unfinished, improvised and provisional. These qualities of open-endedness and contradiction are qualities to be embraced, in the full spirit of such an ambitious collaboration and so will, I believe, complement the overall objective of enabling a memorable and provocative learning experience for the students.

In essence, in relation to what we might describe as Sillman's and Owens' 'cultivated cack-handedness'—which takes risks in a humorous move to push the potential of painting and simultaneously destabilises a patriarchal tradition—Mark's recent work takes parallel risks by presenting an affirmatively generous form of 'unfinished', 'provisional' and 'improvised' painting, with a corresponding levelling of taste, alongside a simultaneous deep engagement with the role of the artist as a historical educator and producer of knowledge.

Moreover, Mark's work also enters into another self-conscious system of discourse around an alternative network of painting. Instead of linking to an ironic institutional-critical network of artists, his current work connects to contentious contemporary issues of 'self-taught', 'naïve', 'folk' and 'outsider' painting, all of which are categories that exist within separate and connected traditions in their own right within the institution of wider contemporary painting.

In the 2019 survey exhibition of contemporary Australian art in Sydney at The National, for example, collaborative works by Selma Nunay Coulthard, Noreen Hudson, and Clara, Reinhold and Vanessa Inkamala, such as *Mparra Karrti—Us mob belong to the Country* (2018–19), show participatory traditions beyond the Western canon as a post-digital photographic-painterly practice. Similarly, in the 2019 exhibition *Rhoda Kellogg*, curated by Brian Belott at White Columns, we see the power of children's art in the clinical psychologist's seminal work pioneering its use for studying child development. Here Kellogg appears as a revolutionary who attempted to expand an appreciation of a misunderstood genre. Belott states:

> Rhoda Kellogg (1898–1987) is an American hero who dedicated her life to a field of study that remains severely underappreciated some forty years later: early childhood art. Kellogg showed the highest regard for an age group who normally are the first to be ushered off a sinking boat, but once upon dry land are the first to be shuffled out of sight, out of the way so that the adult world can continue with its own agenda. What amazes me is the zone of confusion child art has always occupied. It is worthless, yet priceless. The contemporary art world cannot figure out how to commodify it, yet it is the source

of all art and language. It has been proven to be a central inspiration for some of art history's top modernists, but it is worth nothing when a four-year-old does similar work with equal competence.[3]

In an analogous manner to the paradox of taking 'naïve' yet simultaneously sophisticated work seriously, Mark's work with young people is deliberately offered up to be misconstrued as a school project, a fact that reveals a deeply critical site that intentionally jars with the market's ability to commodify a community painting made by children. This also relates somewhat to the tension contained in historical institutional commissions in public discourse being made again, this time not as a private commodity (connected to the third-party producer in terms of portraiture, patronage in the public sector and systems of authority at work in the image). The Sistine Chapel is an example of this (relating to art and government as oppositional to painting's connection with the market). In this respect, the work connects the commercial and public spheres in an awkward manner, again in an analogue field of painting during our ongoing technological revolution and its accelerated effects on human behaviour related to current forms of stress-reality.

Historically speaking then, this painting is a radically minor small-scale experiential learning process that connects to the historical context provided by the 'artist's studio', where history paintings were conceived and made by the artist in tandem with a team of assistants. The fundamental position that seems to remain is that this image of community art in the digital age operates in a relaxed space or gap between painting and cosmetic imagery. Perhaps we can look at this work as a form of extreme humanity in a world of superficial profundity. If painting is the expert medium of the surface, then this isn't the encrusted surface of a Rembrandt, nor the flat mirror of the digital in Guyton but somewhere in between, an image that contains a superficiality and depth in the public sphere.

---

3   See whitecolumns.org, exhibitions, 2019, Rhoda Kellogg—organised by Brian Belott (accessed 12 May 2020).

In the field
Helen Carey

The independent curator is often poised between sensing great potential to address complex and timely subjects and navigating invisible borders that reduce their capacity to develop significant output with the minimal assets with which they are equipped. They pursue subjects by maintaining a serious, persuasive passion for their projects alongside a committed focus on supporting participating artists as well as other collaborators along the way. Independent curators are positioned in the field, which is often imagined as the inverse of the academy. The field is interpreted to be an arena where freedom to explore is unbounded by institutional rules and where organisation is often an uncomfortable limit.

However, a contradiction arises in this relationship between field and academy: the production of knowledge in the field has become more and more formalised, and yet if the academy tries to work with the field, it attempts to be looser and more fluid, with no clear framework. We often observe these patterns in the design of curatorial programmes developed by universities, in the work of independent practitioners who enter the academic system as visiting lecturers, or in the efforts of artists who work to develop joint publications with academics.

Thinking in both interdisciplinary and transdisciplinary terms, perhaps these two arenas of knowledge production—the field and the academy—will veer closer together and develop interfaces that allow a functional hybrid—a third arena—to emerge. In order for this to occur, those who are positioned as gatekeepers within the academy will need to provide access to their resources, while independent practitioners who operate within the field will need to clearly articulate the perspectives that they have developed. In looking at how these two arenas interface, a means of instigating new forms of knowledge generation in a rapidly changing world that allows (and even encourages) cross-fertilisation between diverse arenas of endeavour might be developed.

Interface

In 2017, the Irish commissioning agency Create, the National College of Art and Design (NCAD) and Fire Station Artists' Studios (FSAS), where I currently work as director, undertook an ambitious project exploring the interfaces between the field and the academy. The resulting publication *TransActions #2: Field and Academy: Knowledge and Counter-knowledge in Socially Engaged Art* (2016) examined practice and potential in the field of contemporary art, drawing different perspectives from artists, academics, educators and other arts professionals.[1]

What became evident through this project conference was that it primarily focused on the academy, and on how knowledge production was frequently compromised by an internal struggle concerning accounting, administration and curriculum development. Notwithstanding the presence of many practitioners who work independently, the discussions that developed both formally and informally throughout the conference did little to highlight the wider field as similarly complex; the concerns of the academy were treated as more urgent. Similarly, although its theme was defined as 'knowledge and counter-knowledge', the conference spent little time questioning the ideas behind socially engaged art practice itself—a difficult practice to define—focusing instead on a lack of resources and difficulties arising within personal research methodologies, with entrenched oppositions arising between different interest groups.

There are many probable reasons why the conference narrowed its scope in this way, but the result was that the substance of the mode through which socially engaged arts practice is understood or articulated was obstructed. Both the publication in its content and the conference

---

[1] NCAD participated in this publication through its MA in Socially Engaged Art. See Jennie Guy, 'How People Come Up With Ideas', in *TransActions #2 Field and Academy: Knowledge and Counter-knowledge in Socially Engaged Art* (Dublin: NCAD, Fire Station Artists' Studios and Create, 2017).

in what was covered highlighted that this field and its corresponding institutions struggle to identify terms for engaging with each other, to articulate their areas of common interest, and to agree on consistent terms of reference.

Methodology

The fluid nature of how the field operates can be slippery to work with when positioned against the formal frameworks of other structures of knowledge generation. When examined against the backdrop of peer review and mechanisms for publication within the academy, for instance, the field does not possess established frameworks; instead it relies on experimentation and sui generis methods that evade interrogation.

Perhaps in addressing this, the field has shifted towards establishing frameworks with characteristics that mimic—perhaps repurpose—those of the academy. For example, within socially engaged arts practice, it is often suggested now as best practice to develop standards for consulting constituencies from whom information is gathered, such as with Fiona Reilly's current work *The Department of Time Keepers*.[2] Through such processes, the gathering of empirical data becomes more robust, and behavioural conclusions are tested and defended.

Another example of using formal methodologies is *The Market* (2013), where artist Mark Curran draws on methodologies of data analysis related to risk taking in banking behaviour. Pursuing algorithmic methods that are forensic in character, Curran places a robust foundation alongside the substantive claim that algorithms render decisions unchangeable, even in the face of crisis. He augments this by granting the work accessibility in a sculptural and sound dimension that situates the work equally within a more formal art tradition as well as

[2] Fiona Reilly's work can be seen at fionareilly.info.

within an academic, political science context whose methods to generate work are used. And yet, in order for this work to be referenced by the academy it must qualify as a reliable source along academic lines in order for it to be cited.

For this integration to take place, a project such as Curran's would have to self-consciously acknowledge that it has absorbed many of the methodologies and constraints of the academy, and in that process, shed any image of the risk and experimentation affiliated with artistic production in the past. Perhaps through such an acceptance of this loss, practitioners whose work occupies this space between the field and the academy might produce new insights and catalyse the development of a hybrid that emerges through entirely different sources of knowledge, sampling from a variety of formal characteristics.

Soft Knowledge

Something that has informed my own practice is that instinct, emotion, experience and absurdity actively contribute to new work. Whether it is an object or an immersive experience, the production of work which succeeds in communicating the incommunicable has been attributed to alchemy, to magic and to an elusive quality that the figure of the artist might channel. The freedom and subjectivity inherent in this has often been resisted as a platform that can yield significant and reliable conclusions on which to make decisions that affect society. The principle is that this is not a hard, verifiable form of knowledge: instead, it might be considered as a form of soft, perhaps resistible knowledge.

Artist Anthony Haughey examined the scars of the financial crisis in his photographic work *Settlement* (2017), and Duncan Campbell's film *Arbeit* (2011)[3] looks at the thinking of German economist Hans Tietmayer in Germany, the Deutsche Mark and Euro, and the movement

3 Duncan Campbell, Irish Museum of Modern Art, 2014.
4 The 1913 Lockout (26 August 1913–18 January 1914) was a general strike led by union leader Jim Larkin which started when transport employers under the leadership of William Martin Murphy attempted to bar workers from joining the Irish Transport and General Workers Union.

of capital. These two artists look at knowledge through works that draw simultaneously on the irrefutable facts of what actually occurred, on hard imagery and on the emotional responses infused therein. Haughey's presentation of a landscape scarred by housing constructions that are abandoned unfinished uses light and formal composition that infuses the banal scene with melancholy and heartbreak, imagining and broken dreams. Campbell presents the notion of currency alongside the society that it will impact through policy decisions about money, giving economic ideas power over a human landscape.

The emotional reactions produced through these works engender soft knowledge. However, the visual language and devices through which these works can be experienced and even how the works are articulated are often seen as a barrier to admitting this soft knowledge as having an important contribution to decision-making. At the same time, the academy requires translation of work originating in the field into an academic framework within which it simply does not fit. These barriers between soft knowledge and decision-making are significant challenges for contemporary art to address.

Independence

In 2009, I hosted *Three Forum*, looking at how the state could approach commemorations of the 1913 Lockout.[4] These events were the first steps in developing exhibitions for what would be among the first in a decade of commemorations for Ireland. As an independent curator working without a supporting institution, I worked to convene a coalition of interest groups—from the unions to labour historians—to make a case for the possibility that art should be a key component in processes for developing commemorations. The event developed as a journey which included approaching various gatekeepers, who guarded groups of enthusiastic potential collaborators—this gatekeeping seems to arise from the need to protect but also from the competitive spirit of funding and influencing.

In this scenario, working as an independent practitioner equipped me with a freedom to make decisions, but limited my ability to specify what sites and budgets I was working with—all elements were relational and contingent at planning stage. While five years of project development (2009–2013) was a substantial lead-in for this project, it was still a tight time frame within which to establish the reputational capital and framework for exhibition opportunities which would hold value for the different collaborators and audiences with whom I was negotiating. This was expensive and took time.

In the resulting exhibition, *Labour and Lockout* in Limerick City Gallery of Art in 2013,[5] another work by Anthony Haughey, *Dispute* (2013), was included. This work marked the sacking of workers on poor terms from Kingscourt's Lagan Brick Factory, which had ceased production due to the economic recession.[6] One day during the exhibition, a visitor and his family came to the gallery. He had been one of the Lagan Brick workers, had heard about the exhibition and about Haughey's process of engagement, and had wanted to come to Limerick to see the exhibition. This connection, one of many unknown connections, sustained in my mind the case for independent work.

Field Work

In consideration of these experiences, separations between or hierarchies of sources of knowledge, gathered from different ecosystems, create a tension that is often unproductive. What the field can give to the academy, and the academy to the field, must help define a new model of knowledge production for twenty-first-century artwork. It is encouraging to see independent curators, artists and educators, and indeed a hybrid of all

---

5 Helen Carey served as director/curator at Limerick City Gallery of Art, 2012–2014.
6 Lagan Brick workers went on strike for 273 days in 2011, over poor redundancy settlements, which was settled in September 2012.

three, work with this fluid situation, listening to each other and letting each other in. Gatekeeping must find a way to trust, allowing more movement between fields of endeavour.

This fluidity manifests within the exhibition *It's Very New School* curated by Jennie Guy at Rua Red in 2017. This exhibition forms a dialogue between the work of six artists who have been involved with Guy's project Art School, navigating through disparate spheres of activity as a sort of testing ground that traverses the boundaries between field work and the idea of curriculum.[7] From the perspective of the academy, the educational curriculum progresses through stages of learning: how to learn and to socialise, the cornerstones of established knowledge, how to interrogate this knowledge, and eventually (in advanced education) learning how to formulate new knowledge. It is along this trajectory that students fall off or move on. The standards of the curriculum are calibrated to enable it to continue and to develop, while keeping new knowledge—that originates from outside of the academy, perhaps—to a minimum. This model can be seen as a pyramid, in which learning starts from a wide base and finishes in a sharp apex, carved from a wider context that is chaotic and unruly, and where enormous knowledge exists in raw form.

The methodology of the academic curriculum is to make the route safe and predictable. *It's Very New School* proposes a form of curriculum that operates according to another logic. It asserts that providing such a sanitised encounter with knowledge production is something that artists resist. Instead, actively engaging with artistic production continuously suggests that there is more that we do not access. These forms of research and production are particularly sensitive to the knowledge that is active and relevant to our times. With the government of Ireland so committed to creativity as a cornerstone of how children and young people achieve their potential,[8] a curriculum for these times should be open to engaging with the unruly potential of the field—through the work of artists—and

---

7   *It's Very New School*, curated by Jennie Guy, featured works by John Beattie, Ella de Búrca, Sarah Browne, Priscila Fernandes, Maria McKinney, Mark O'Kelly and Sarah Pierce.

8   *Creative Youth, Creative Ireland Programme 2017–22*, Department of Education and Skills, Ireland, 2017.

not tethered to the rules of the status quo or defined in terms that are all too clearly defined and understood by those in power.

In a recent public talk in Trinity College Dublin's Long Room,[9] discussions around an access programme and how it can reach disenfranchised young people focused on entrance into the academy. It asked how we might best enable a young person from a challenged background to enter the university system. Through these discussions, it became clear that the academy has to realise that entry into this system is not necessarily an ambition for these young people or indeed for young people in general, if such an offer does not equip them with what they need to exist in the fast-paced context in which they live. Indeed, the academy and the field need to meet, across disciplines. Young people are setting these terms, and after all, the future belongs to them.

---

9 'Trinity and the Changing City: Social Class in Dublin: The Final Taboo', Trinity Long Room Hub, 4 April 2019.

Weird science
Hannah Jickling and Helen Reed

Part 1—Life, Uh, Finds a Way

We usually arrive at Queen Alexandra Elementary School about twenty or thirty minutes before the end of lunch hour. We've been artists-in-residence at this school for about four years, coming once or twice a week to create projects with student groups.[1] The brick building is on a concrete lot, surrounded by a chain-link fence, kitty corner to a Chevron station and a busy bus stop. We see some of the students crossing the street to buy a Slurpee or candy from the gas station shop, travelling in packs of three or four.

The front doors are especially busy at lunchtime; kids drift in and out. A lone child sits on the steps, reading a book or playing a game. Occasionally a student will hold the door open for us. More often, we open the doors to an outgoing flood of children.

On our way to the office we pass a collaboratively painted mural of the schoolyard and the student display case, which showcases classroom projects. This month it features modelling-clay dinosaurs battling on construction paper landscapes. Some of the dinosaurs are recognisable—a tyrannosaurus, a triceratops, a brontosaurus. Others are more free form, a creature with a walrus body and a duck head, or something that looks like a collapsed yellow snowman. The assignment was to create a model based on an actual dinosaur, but, as Dr Ian Malcolm (Jeff Goldblum) noted in the 1993 adventure science fiction film *Jurassic Park*, 'Life, uh, finds a way.' In the context of Jurassic Park, Dr Malcolm is suggesting that the living world will always behave beyond your imagination. In the context of the elementary school, assignments are transcended and new forms hatch.

[1] *Big Rock Candy Mountain* is a public artwork by Hannah Jickling and Helen Reed sited in an East Vancouver elementary school, produced by Other Sights for Artists' Projects.

Outside the office there's an untouched bowl of fresh apples and inside there are a few children slumped in chairs, icing a bruise, waiting for a parent or talking through a tantrum with a support worker. Staff and teachers hurry through the office on their way to and from the staff room. Sometimes we chat with the receptionist, but often there are so many bodies scurrying around that we just sign ourselves in and head upstairs.

The classroom door has been left open for us so that we can set up. Usually we're carrying lots of supplies—an IKEA bag full of printmaking tools, a box of off-brand gum, collage materials, an assortment of glue sticks. The room is usually dishevelled. Desk surfaces are covered in hand-drawn comics, textbooks, water bottles, Shopkins, stickers and homemade stress balls. Someone has written and triple underlined 'CALMING ISLAND' on the chalkboard over the carpet area. The walls are plastered with informative posters, completed worksheets, schedules and affirmative slogans in bubble letters: 'It's a great day to learn something new.' A few stray pencil crayons lie on the floor. A student has a separate desk area with magnetic sand where he will play for most of the class period.

We have about twenty minutes to get set up before the group comes in. We create stations, lay out supplies, set up the projector. There is a loud buzz, and the doors rattle open and close, footsteps in the halls, laughter, chatting, yelling. The students trickle in one by one, and hang up their bags and jackets. A few come to chat with us—'What are we doing today?' 'Are we going to work on prints like last week?' 'Can I try that gum?' A second loud buzz means that they must take their seats while announcements are run through on the PA system. These are read by an upper level student, and include information about what time the basketball team is to meet, where Writers' Room will be held, and who needs to come to the office for undeclared reasons. A student quietly gets up and descends the stairs. He does not return for the rest of the day.

For a number of years, we've centred our practice in and around spaces of schooling, particularly the public elementary school. Public schools are endlessly weird, disturbing, fascinating and everything in between. There is joy, subversion, control, kindness, chaos, bullying and friendship. In *Big Rock Candy Mountain*, we work with the children to research taste and flavour, both gustatory and cultural. We position this investigation in the public-school system as a seat of taste-making. It's one of the first places that we might encounter different values from our family of origin, and that we might learn about all of the complications of sharing public space.

Part 2—
Question: What do you think an artist does? Answer: DRUGS![2]

Maria McKinney is talking with Fourth Class students at St Mary's National School in Maynooth, Co. Kildare—a video recording reveals a familiar commotion in the space of a classroom. The artist continues to enquire: What is art and what forms can it take? Can you make art for an animal? Or with an animal? The artist and the class are creating sculptures together, elaborate perches imagined for birds of prey, as part of an Art School residency. The process of *Birds of Prey* begins with a tactile exploration of bird forms. Each student creates a set of ten paper talons, which they place on their fingertips and gesture with, attempt to pick up their pencils, attempt to turn the pages of books with much difficulty.

Birds of Prey is related to another body of McKinney's work called *Sire*, a series of woven sculptures temporarily mounted on the backs of live bulls and documented in photographs. The sculptures are artistic transductions of genetic information into colourful, geometric

---

[2] Conversation transcribed from video of Maria McKinney presenting to the class of students at St Mary's National School. Jennie Guy, 'Birds of Prey HD', YouTube video (accessed 12 May 2020).

forms built from brightly coloured semen straws, the vessels used for the artificial insemination process. Each sculpture references qualities that have been intentionally bred into cows. As she advances through slides of this project, a chorus of 'wooooooah', 'oooooh', 'that one's nice' erupts from the class.

The helix forms of *Sire* echo the braided shapes of the pre-Christian craft of corn dollies. Corn dollies were created from cereal crop straws as a symbol of fertility, a material emblem of hope for a successful harvest the subsequent year.[3] McKinney's *Sire* takes up this human desire for a bountiful harvest by collapsing the folkloric aesthetics of the corn dollies with the intentional genetic manipulation through line breeding practices. In *Sire*, the corn straw is replaced with the plastic straws used in line breeding practices.

Line breeding is the practice of interbreeding within a line of descent to concentrate specific traits into a herd. The Belgian Blue cow, one of the subjects of *Sire*, has a particular gene mutation which results in a huge amount of muscle growth. The myostatin gene ('myo' meaning muscle and 'statin' meaning stop) has been effectively bred out of the cow. The Belgian Blue's muscles will grow forever, without a gym membership, protein shakes or steroids. The human benefit being a more affordable source of lean beef.

Part 3—Molecules of Desire

A flavourist looking to create a strawberry flavour for an ice cream may not want to recreate an entire strawberry molecule by molecule, but instead *author* a strawberry that emphasises certain flavour notes that are appropriate for an ice cream.[4] The flavourist handcrafts molecules of desire into a sensation for consumers. Science historian Nadia Berenstein writes about the design and manipulation of flavour at the molecular level

---

[3] Bridget Haggerty, 'Putting out the hare, putting on the harvest knots', available at irishcultureandcustoms.com (accessed 18 April 2019).

[4] Nadia Berenstein, 'Welcome to Flavor Country', public lecture, Western Front Gallery, Vancouver, British Columbia, 7 November 2018.

in her research on the history of flavour design. This history begins in the late 1800s, as food and agriculture become increasingly industrialised, with the first ever artificial flavour created in the 1870s. Flavour additives start to become more common, not just because of changing methods of production and processing, but also because of consumer behaviour; molecularly modified flavour keeps the consumer coming back.[5]

In *Big Rock Candy Mountain*, we work with school-age children to research the ways that our own senses of taste and distinction develop. There are many food products that directly attempt to address young people. Candy and junk food, for example. Adults make all kinds of distinctions between good and bad gustatory tastes. Particularly when it comes to children's own choices of food. As adults, we might encourage fresh fruits and vegetables, offer apple slices for dessert. But often, after having acquired some pocket money, a child's first purchase will be candy—super-sour Toxic Waste from the convenience store, or chewy Airheads. When kids get a chance to make their own decision, based on their own desires, candy is the choice that they will frequently make. Allison James notes this phenomenon in her article 'Confections, Concoctions and Conceptions' (1982), in which she discusses the way that the purchase of candy is a way to express a childhood desire outside the bounds of watchful adult eyes and interests.[6]

Flavour design, like the line breeding practices in the creation of Belgian Blue cows, is a process of the contemporary food system that is largely invisible to consumers. This deliberate crafting at the molecular level creates a particular sensory experience. Tastes and textures are designed, in the effort to satisfy a competitive food market that demands low prices and distinct flavour profiles. In McKinney's *Sire*, an audience is able to consider the crafting of the genetic sequences of the bulls that wear her sculptures. At St Mary's National School, the students viewing *Sire* can begin a conversation about the more abstract processes of cattle

---

[5] Nadia Berenstein, 'Designing Flavors for Mass Consumption', *The Senses and Society* 13, no. 1 (2018): 19–40.

[6] Allison James, 'Confections, Concoctions and Conceptions', in *The Children's Culture Reader*, ed. Henry Jenkins (New York: NYU Press, 1998), 394–405.

farming. And, through the creation of *Birds of Prey*, can continue to consider the complex interrelationships between humans and animals.

Part 4—Natural and Manufactured

There is a comic absurdity to our current food system—double-muscle cows, a quest for extreme and abstract mystery flavours. How we arrived at this current culinary moment is not easy to comprehend. Industrial food systems are a blend of both organic processes and forceful human intervention. For art practice and production that reflect these hard-to-believe realities, what is the value of encountering these phenomena alongside groups of children? As adults, the social and cultural structures that we live within can become normal, everyday and naturalised. As offered by Jack Halberstam: 'Kid knowledge about life, about embodiment, about art, and about power is rarely cultivated and tends to be cast as a naïve version of what adults already know.'[7] Having to explain 'the way things are' becomes an exercise in noticing the bizarre systems that we create, inhabit and take for granted.

Returning to the fictitious clay dinosaurs from the Queen Alexandra Elementary School display case, the molecularly designed flavours in snack foods, and genetically altered cows, it is tempting to differentiate between what is sanctioned or 'off base', but with closer attention, distinctions between good, bad, fake, real, natural and unnatural are difficult to pin down. In the case of *Big Rock Candy Mountain* productions, and in the presentation of McKinney's work at St Mary's National School, these projects frustrate tidy learning outcomes and seek to re-evaluate that which is overlooked, inconvenient or taboo. In these instances, artists and children work together to uncover the nuanced conditions facing future generations of consumers and cultural producers. These encounters should not be understood as populist impulses that

---

[7] Jack Halberstam, 'Everything is Awesome! Children, Legos and the Art of Failure', in *Multiple Elementary*, eds. Hannah Jickling and Helen Reed (Toronto: Black Dog Publishing and YYZ Books, 2017), 32–7.

flatten perspective and potential; rather we should strive to preserve the weirdness, idiosyncrasies and complexities that move art discourse forward. Through our encounter with McKinney's work as part of Art School, we are delighted to find ourselves in good company—asserting the classroom as an exhibition space, entertaining the curricular as a curatorial endeavour and exploring new forms of being and thinking together. Ultimately, these gestures advocate for the critical presence of young people in the co-creation of meaning that surrounds contemporary art production.

The masterplan
Juan Canela

Universities and art schools are currently in a state of emergency in the European Union because of the Bologna Process[1]—whose consequences include privatisation, economic cuts, increases in fees and degradations of the academic and intellectual environment—but also because of a paradigm shift in the teacher–student relationship due to students' ability to access a lot of knowledge simply on their mobile phone. In addition, artistic training is slowly disappearing from formal mandatory education, both primary and secondary, as specialised courses on contemporary art, for artists as well as curators and scholars, are proliferating everywhere.[2]

In the Spanish context, a series of measures adopted within the LOMCE (Organic Law 8/2013, of 9 December, for the improvement of educational quality), show a clear tendency to relegate the arts, humanities and social sciences to a secondary tier in the school curricula versus other subjects (such as language, mathematics and science) identified as 'instrumental', basic competences.[3] The PISA report of the OECD strongly recommends raising the levels of demand for these 'instrumental' subjects to achieve a more competitive workforce. José Ignacio Wert, the Spanish Education Minister who promoted the law, justified this decision by declaring: 'There are subjects that distract.'

It is difficult to find primary and secondary schools where students can be close to contemporary art practice. They might know about Picasso, but most of them won't know about what it really means to be an artist today. Furthermore, this does not concern the study of art alone; art can be an essential ally in the development of the students as political and social subjects.

Art and education hybridise, fostering all kinds of encounters, none of which are instrumental, but instead generate unpredictable and

---

[1] The Bologna Process was initiated after the Bologna Declaration, an agreement reached on 19 June 1999 by the Ministers of Education of twenty-nine European countries (both from the European Union and from other countries such as Russia or Turkey) in the Italian city of Bologna, after its planning, since 1998, in six conferences of ministers in different European cities: Paris (at the Sorbonne University), Bologna, Prague, Berlin, Bergen, London and Leuven/Louvain-la-Neuve (EACEA, 2011).

inseparable forms of creation and learning. Education interrogates art by displacing its dominant disciplinary readings, placing it in relation to other subjectivities, social contexts and political debates, and it also becomes a space of cultural production and creativity in its own right. On the other hand, artistic practice pushes the limits of what has traditionally been understood as the production and transmission of knowledge, exploring the uncertainty of meaning and methodological heterodoxy, while questioning the forms of scientific validity. Maybe we need more subjects that distract.

In this light, the questions that the students of the Dublin 7 Educate Together National School have been addressing in the context of *The Masterplan* project gain relevance:

> *What is school for? What was school for? And what will school be for?*

The Masterplan was a community-based arts initiative that took place during May–June 2016. Organised by curator Jennie Guy, artists John Beattie and Ella de Búrca developed different workshops with the students of Dublin 7 Educate Together National School. The school was temporarily located in Grangegorman Lower, and will be relocated on the new site as part of the area's redevelopment.[4] This movement, which is part of a new city urban plan that involves the relocation of people, frames the development of the project:

> For two centuries or so, Grangegorman was a place to avoid. Few ventured behind the high walls of the old asylum on Dublin's northside, which, at its peak, housed up to 2,000 patients. This largely hidden side of Ireland seemed to function as a closed, confined space,

---

[2] Postgraduate programmes at universities such as Goldsmiths in London, the Dutch Art Institute in the Netherlands or Institut Kunst in Basel; training programmes for artists and curators linked to museums and art centres such as the Postgraduate Study Program (PEI) at MACBA Barcelona or the Whitney Museum Independent Study Program; online courses such as NODE Center in Berlin; and independent or alternative programmes such as BAR Tool in Barcelona or Open East School in London.

cut off from the rest of society. Today, this vast walled-in and unknown part of the city is being opened up. A new urban quarter is slowly taking shape—as host to the biggest higher-education project in the history of the State. Over the coming years, some 20,000 students will be based at Dublin Institute of Technology's sprawling new campus.[5]

One of the main aims of the project was to let the students reflect on how the city changes, the implications of those changes, or the role of their school within the process.

As a curator, the relation between art and education has been a key aspect of my practice. In 2013–14 I had the opportunity of collaborating in Barcelona with Creators IN RESIDENCE, a pioneering programme in Spain aimed at bringing contemporary art to state secondary schools through direct, continuous contact between an artist and students. In this programme, artists are invited to conceive a work that they will then produce together with a group of compulsory secondary education students.[6] Over the academic year, as part of the school timetable, these pupils take part in the conception and creation of the work. No doubt it has been one of the more intense, complex and rich experiences of my career. It offered me the possibility to work directly in an educational context—two Barcelona high schools—and to develop projects with an expanded time frame (an academic year in each case), with a rhythm and a work structure atypical for an art context, and in an environment (a high school) unfamiliar to the artist.

Working with Catalan artists Jaume Ferrete and Lúa Coderch in two different high schools, one of the first things that we learned was that the artist does not have to become a teacher. Instead, the encounter provides sustained exposure to contemporary art practices and theories

---

3   See reference number BOE-A-2013-12886 at boe.es, published 10 December 2013 (accessed 12 May 2020).
4   As stated on the Grangegorman Development Agency's official website. Grangegorman is a new urban quarter being created in Dublin's north inner city. It will have health, education and community at its heart and will open up a once walled off part of Dublin.
5   Carl O'Brien, 'Welcome to Dublin's new urban quarter', *Irish Times*, 7 April 2018.
6   For more information visit the website enresidencia.org.

for the students. We also learned that we should find different ways of communicating than we are used to. The students are a very particular 'audience', and the school is a very particular 'venue'. When working in a school, you are developing a project inside an institution with a strong hierarchical internal structure, where different norms and regulations function on a day-to-day-life basis. How do you articulate a dialogue with a group of students, who maybe are not interested in what you want to tell them, inside this sometimes too rigid environment?

Alongside Jaume Ferrete we worked with a First Year group (12–13-year-old students) from a suburban neighbourhood in Barcelona. The idea was to work around performance practice and the political implications of the voice, but we quickly realised that their attention spans were very short, and that they just wanted to go home. So we began to invite different people to the classes, and went out to visit different museums, exhibitions or performances. Going to a new place or meeting someone new renewed their attention. It was a long process to understand how to engage with the students, and how to establish a dialogue with them. We ended up developing a performance programme in the gym, in which the content and format of each session was a collective decision, and we invited the public to each session. Learning by doing and giving them agency in the decision-making were very important aspects in that process.

This empowerment is also present in Beattie and de Búrca's working process at Dublin 7 Educate Together National School. They developed with the students a series of performance works both non-verbal and choral, creating a collaborative and dialogical space for the students to shape their own voices. If usually they are habituated to solve problems with a correct answer following an unanswerable logic, thinking along dualities that are related with good or bad, yes or no, correct or incorrect, Beattie and de Búrca introduced in the group the possibility of thinking and imagining from a subjective sphere. The group developed a spoken-word opera built around the questions quoted above, and these open, subjective questions allowed them to explore uncertainty. Performing on the site where the school will be located allowed them to connect directly with that site, with the movement of the student bodies becoming part of its development. They created hand gestures to coordinate written sentences that reflect the past, present and future of the school. The event evolved as a performative time capsule that allowed the students to imagine different perspectives on this landscape and city, and their presence within them—to be aware of their capacity as political subjects.

In the second phase of *The Masterplan*, entitled *I'll Be In Your Camp—Will You Be In Mine?*, Naomi Sex and Karl Burke (artists and lecturers in the Technological University Dublin) worked to establish a close dialogue with the students of St Paul's CBS Secondary School. Naomi Sex developed a workshop in which the students could use different materials and tools in the university facilities to work in printmaking techniques. Giving them access to the machines and the knowledge on how to use them empowered not only the students, allowing them to generate different graphics, but also the local community, opening up access to particular technical and material resources to a broader student public. In our digital age it offered the students a much-needed change; sharing these manual techniques allowed them to better understand the importance of material processes and how they related to their bodies. Karl Burke developed a workshop where they experimented with sculptural techniques using day-to-day materials. The students learned about structure, collaboration and spatiality through installation. Using the tables, chairs and other classroom elements, they were able to change the use of their classroom, challenging the spatial and architectural environment.

The Masterplan is one of those projects whose roots are entangled in that strong and complex knot moulded by the relation between art and education. Both share the intention of helping to elucidate what we don't know, challenge our understanding of reality, provoke learning processes and transform people and their contexts.[7] But even if they share different aspects, it is clear that both spheres belong to different contexts running under different forms of operability. Developing the project in the schools with the students highlights one of the key aspects of this intersection: the difference between learning as a process that is encountered in all areas of life (maybe closer to art practices) and the more top-down or institutionalised educational processes (maybe closer to formal education). As Annette Krauss writes, knowledge and education are liberating, but also restricting, so how can we deal with this ambiguity and paradox when it comes to actual practices?[8] And another pertinent question, also related to the particular context in which *The Masterplan* has been developed: how could we learn to not be compliant, functioning agents of a dominant social and economic system, but create the possibility for critical voices to appear? We need to develop projects and initiatives in our schools and pedagogical institutions whose processes not only share artistic knowledge with the students, but also infect all their learning structures. We should open the methods and the objectives to the intervention of those who act as guides. And we should find ways of generating processes of proximity among the different agents involved, offering empowerment to the students and opening space for uncertainty when becoming political subjects.

---

7   Another interesting project dealing with this same relation is *Ni arte ni educación*, an exhibition and program of activities run by the Grupo de Educación de Matadero Madrid, which explored zones of contact between art and education in 2015.

8   A. Krauss, E. Pethick and M. Vishmidt, 'Spaces of Unexpected Learning', in *Curating and the Educational Turn*, eds. Paul O'Neill and Mick Wilson (London: Open Editions, 2010).

Dear revolutionary teacher…

Sofía Olascoaga and Priscila Fernandes

Although we haven't met you yet, we were hoping we might communicate with you through this section in *Curriculum*. We are sending you a set of letters accompanied by questions and exercises that can be used in a classroom to tap into conversations with your students. We hope that these connect to your daily teaching experiences, and the potential for these exchanges to be transformative of subjects and worldviews.

The themes we would like to share are derived from the installation *A friend in common* that was commissioned for the exhibition *It's Very New School*, which emerged through the Art School platform in 2017.[1] This installation was the result of Priscila's sustained interest in the Modern School (*Escuela Moderna*), a primary school for children and their parents that existed between 1901 and 1909 in Barcelona, Spain.

The elements that we are sending you here stem from a conversation between the two of us, which was triggered by *A friend in common* and nourished by our own educational experiences. It has evolved as a means of sharing our mutual concerns related to current school contexts for artistic and teaching practices.

We should begin by explaining how the Modern School became such an important focus for Priscila's wonderings.

The Industrial Revolution brought about an increasingly organised working class capable of furnishing its own forms of education. Francisco Ferrer i Guàrdia, a Catalan pedagogue working at the turn of the twentieth century, exemplifies the historical tendency to base such initiatives on modern principles such as rationality, science and equality. While only active for less than a decade, Ferrer's Modern School in Barcelona was exceptionally productive of radical thought, yet none of this seemed dedicated to art, despite several articles published in its monthly newsletter that pointed to the role of the artist in society and the advantages of including artistic activities in the learning process.[2]

As Priscila was researching about this revolutionary educational

---

1 *It's Very New School* is an exhibition that took place between 4 March and 22 April 2017 at Rua Red, South Dublin Arts Centre (Tallaght, Ireland). The exhibition was curated by Jennie Guy, and featured work from artists John Beattie, Sarah Browne, Ella de Búrca, Priscila Fernandes, Mark O'Kelly, Maria McKinney and Sarah Pierce. The majority of these works drew from Art School workshops and residencies that these artists had been involved in.

2 The Modern School published more than forty books and school manuals in an attempt

programme, she was curious about this conspicuous absence of art, and ventured to fill in the blank. Taking the principles of the Modern School, she started developing a map linking authors and artists that could be sympathetic or in dialogue with the ideological affiliations of the programme. That compilation resulted in *The Book of Aesthetic Education of the Modern School*, an exhibition which initiates activities and debates relating to art education.[3]

The installation *A friend in common* takes this research a step further, by presenting fictionalised correspondence between Ferrer and prominent artists of the early twentieth century. These intimate letters anchor the radical art movement within a politically turbulent era, when fascism was on the rise across Europe and World War I was on the horizon. This correspondence attempts to cross the ideology of the Modern School with the positions of early twentieth-century artists, a gesture that makes us consider the role of the artist in the shaping of an art curriculum. By doing that, the letters advance important debates around revolutionary discourses and structural contradictions of the educational field, diverse ideological approaches, power dynamics, positions and gender relationships between school founders, staff and promoters—or even in relation to art and artists.

Priscila created gestural ink drawings which then were exhibited side by side with the letters as the installation *A friend in common* within *It's Very New School*, which comprised pieces by other artists who had intervened directly in educational spaces, working with local schools and students. However, the letters and questions that constitute *A friend in common* have yet to make their way back to an actual school.

The Modern School can be an inspiration to rethink revolutionary forces in education. Priscila's approach to intersecting with the school through *A friend in common* provides an excuse to expand our own imaginary on art, education and radical thinking. We believe that the

---

to break away from other school programmes they considered incoherent. In this collection of red pocket-sized books are titles focused on the natural and social sciences, alongside books focused on arithmetic, universal history and psychology. Other titles were more ideologically charged, offering a critical standpoint on patriotism and colonialism, the 'horrors of war, and the iniquity of conquest'. Literary pieces depicted 'social evils', such as *Las Aventuras de Nono* (The Adventures of Nono) by Jean Grave, a story about a boy travelling through the country of Autonomy, a utopian place where boys and girls are equal, where there is no ill-treatment or punishment and where one can enjoy freedom. In the country of Autonomy, the names of the story's characters

natural cycle of this interrogative impulse may only be completed if it manages to resonate again within an actual educational context. This is our motivation: to use these part-fact/part-fiction exchanges between artists and educators of the Modern School as tools to reflect on contemporary educational narratives and urgencies in this field. Thus our outreach to you, as a wave that may resonate with your own experience.

In the following pages, you will find some of the original letters developed for *A friend in common* set in dialogue with questions and exercises which propose new modes of engaging with them. It is our hope that the colloquial reflections offered by the writers, and by our interlocution with their words, may be of interest to your teaching practice and might seep into your own classroom conversations. Rather than engaging in a historical overview of the Modern School, we believe some of the questions—both real and fictional—posed by the constellation of friends, workers, intellectuals, ideologists, artists, members and founders of the school may resonate deeply with how we think of education today.

As cultural agents, as educators, as artists and as curators, we have reflected upon the processes that unfold in the transit between on the one hand school spaces, classrooms and groups of students, and on the other art spaces such as exhibition rooms, art museums and art schools. We find that our daily practices of teaching, learning and creating continuously intersect with these questions, and we hope they may resonate with you as well.

In the hope that some further channels allow our voices to connect, we leave you with the questions we've found along the way.

Warmly,
Priscila and Sofía
From Rotterdam and Mexico City
July 2019

---

give us an insight into its ideological charge: Solidarity, Sincerity, Freedom and Labour.

3 *The Book of Aesthetic Education of the Modern School* was first exhibited at Espai 13, Fundació Joan Miró, as part of the exhibition cycle *Lesson 0*, curated by Juan Canela and Ane Aguirre. It has since travelled to the Reykjavik Museum (Iceland), ENT (Rotterdam, The Netherlands) and Kunsthall Stavanger (Norway). For more information visit priscilafernandes.net, 2014, The Book of Aesthetic Education of the Modern School (accessed 12 May 2020).

FRIEND FERRER,

My anguish, my suffering, my pain of every sort when I heard you have fallen victim of such unjust accusation and that you could be facing a death sentence for the crime of rebellion. It is ludicrous. This is a judicial crime, perfidiously planned by vengeful enemies of your school. How can I contact your lawyer? I want to place my testimony before the court and do everything at my reach. Dear Francisco, accept the help of he who declares himself to be your entirely devoted friend and tell me how to proceed.

There can be no doubt that the revolution of the Neo-Impressionists is peaceful, as is yours. We are not interested in violence or anarchy as a means of revolt. We want instead to imagine a dreamed-of age of happiness through our paintings, and to depict scenes where there are no hierarchies, where there is no private property and people live a more natural form of existence, sharing all the means of production while having an individual autonomy within the collective. This is the real progress we want to achieve.

My heroic friend, I repeat that I am an affectionate supporter of the Modern School and await anxiously your freedom.

P. SIGNAC

From Paul Signac to Francisco Ferrer Guardia, Saint-Tropez, Friday, 8 October 1909

Use Ferrer's figure as a reference to discuss the transformational force of education and political commitment to create better conditions for life and for people. Reflect upon current cases in which educators are repressed.

How are hierarchies perceived by members of your classroom, at home, in society in general?

Who and what defines what constitutes 'a natural form of existence'? What are other forms of existence that may not be considered 'natural'? How do you participate in these forms of existence in your life, school and home?

What is a collective? How do you understand yourself as part of a collective, or as part of several collectives? Who are the other members of these collectives? What do you think is learned, given, taken, created and cultivated within these collectives? Would you be able to learn all of these things by yourself?

What is individual autonomy? How does it relate to being part of a collective?

DEAR MRS. MEUNIER

I can assure you that your funding for The Modern School will be well used. We are ready to open the doors at Calle de Bailén 56, all rooms with fantastic natural light, even a small garden at the back where the children can run freely. So far we have 68 students registered. For the time being I believe it is important to keep it to this modest number so that we can properly develop the content of the courses.

I have devised a programme containing the main ideas for the school, which I am planning to publish soon. This will serve as the guideline for the teachers and possibly to other schools opening abroad. We will also replace all current educational books used for the state curriculum with our own publications—so far we have published *Theory of Evolution* and *Patriotism and Colonization*, which focuses on the evils of nationalist sentiments, colonisation and slavery. We will also publish *Free World* by Jean Grave and a critical book on private property by Pierre-Joseph Proudhon. In this rational and scientific school, far from any dogmatic teaching, our children will be well educated!

To a new generation of freethinkers—to a better future!
F. FERRER

From Francisco Ferrer Guardia to Ernestina Meunier [trustee], Barcelona, Monday, 2 September 1901

What would be included in a syllabus for free-thinkers today? Who would these current free-thinkers be? Political theorists, writers, artists, YouTubers, musicians, activists or other public figures?

How would a free-thinking session take place? Who would compose the space, the dynamic, the format and the elements for a group to pursue these sessions? How would these sessions be constructed? What would the politics of these discussions be?

DEAR FERRER,

I'm sending you the sketch you requested for the book of *Aesthetic Education* of the Modern School. It's my ugliest yet. I entitled it *Étude pour le Café de Nuit* and it's an equivalent to the potato eaters. I've tried to express the terrible human passions with the red and the green.

If I were to give advice to your students it would be to search and paint humanity, humanity and again humanity. To not fall on the decorative for the decorative sake. A thousand times over, one must, even if it's studies of cabbages and salad, represent reality without sacrificing to conventions of beauty or artistry. To create emotions so strong that one might not survive them. To make very ugly paintings.

Ever yours,
VINCENT

From Vincent van Gogh to Francisco Ferrer Guardia, undated

How do we currently understand Humanity?

As a question to the group: What are the components of an ideal notion of Humanity? What are the relationships between this notion of Humanity and other forms of non-human life?

Create individual, small groups or even a larger group composition of images that depict what you've discussed as the ideal representation of Humanity. Place the images in the centre of the room or on a wall where all participants can contemplate them in detail. Provide enough time to observe each of the images created in detail. Initiate a round of conversation on the images. Ask someone who didn't participate in making the images to talk about what they see, or ask the creators to explain their images and how they relate to their thinking.

DEAR FERRER,

Paul Signac—I believe him to be a friend in common—has invited me to spend this summer with him under the spell of Saint-Tropez to compete with each other in some joyous painting *competitions*. For that reason your letter arrived late to me, but I'm glad to finally hear news of your school. It is admirable that the school is rooted in a search for reason and truth. But I should warn you that there are no new truths. The role of the artist, like that of the teacher, consists of seizing current truths often repeated to them, but which will take on new meaning for them and which they will make their own when they grasp their deepest significance.

I remain much obliged to you for your most friendly invitation to come to the Modern School to lecture about my work, but I will have to regrettably decline, or at least on the terms you propose. I do not believe an artist should reveal their ideas on painting to the public. People often assume painting as appendage of literature with specific narrative ideas—this really distresses me. As a matter of fact, I am fully convinced that a painter's best spokesperson is their work.

Instead of coming to teach I would rather send a painting. I have recently completed *Luxe, Calme et Volupté*, in which I have followed the technique of *pointillism* akin to Signac—I will send you this.

At an appropriate moment, invite the students to spend time with the painting and let the work speak for itself. Choose a classroom full of light and provide the students with suitable seating for the viewing, something comfortable, even the floor can be attractive provided you arrange pillows and carpets.

You see what I am after, above all, is expression in terms of arrangement—not the expression of the brush. In a painting every part will play its appointed role: the place occupied by the figures, the empty spaces around them, the proportions, composition—if there is anything that is not useful, then it is harmful to the artwork.

Please send the painting back to Signac, he is expecting to buy it,
Truly yours,

MATISSE

From Henri Matisse to Francisco Ferrer Guardia
Saint-Tropez, Wednesday, 10 August 1904

Who or what defines what is true, and what is 'the truth'? Are there several truths? Are there new truths?

Should we interrogate what is told as truth? What kind of critical skills are needed to initiate dialogue with what may or may not be considered the truths of our times?

How should we sharpen our relationship to what we believe life is, or should be? Should this be informed by what we read online, or what we discuss with our peers, teachers, parents and friends?

How do artists and teachers relate to each other?

What methods could we use to look at an artwork? What questions can we devise in order to understand what we see?

DEAR MR. FERRER,

I would like to organise a visit with your students to the General Exposition in Madrid, where I'm exhibiting the painting <u>La Carga, Barcelona 1902</u> [The Charge]. I would like to have a lively discussion around this work with the students, to bring to the surface awareness and questioning about the crimes being enacted on all citizens of this state, and the authoritarian and violent hand of the police towards its people.

It is through information that change will be possible, and to start with this at a young age is of utmost importance.

Let us make visible these ills so that future progress becomes possible.

Looking forward to hearing from you,
R. CASAS

From Ramon Casas to Francisco Ferrer Guardia
Madrid, Friday, 5 March 1904

The painting *La Carga* represents the repression of the citizens by the state. Find an image of *La Carga*. Discuss its composition and elements.

Can you give examples of current forms of state repression that you are familiar with? Why do these things happen? Who is being repressed, and why? What kind of awareness is currently needed in order to address these situations?

DEAR CLÉMENCE,

I regret that I will no longer be able to teach at the Modern School since I am moving to Paris. The art scene in Barcelona is stagnant and I do not feel energised by this city anymore. Of all that I will leave behind my contact with the school will be the most difficult to give up.

<u>I had always been averse to school when I was a child, I even had fits of rage and panic! For me school seemed like a dead place, and only between my pencils, drawing and looking out the window did I find some consolation.</u> But when I first visited the Modern School I was engulfed by excitement! The absence of coercion, punishment and exams made the children play and learn so freely. Dear Clémence, I felt for the first time in the school I had always dreamed!

I was so delighted when you asked me to teach painting at the Modern School. And I'm equally touched by your caution that this would withdraw precious time from my own creations, but <u>it was perfectly compatible to spend an hour a week without affecting other artistic and worldly commitments</u>. In fact, the contact I had with the children gave me a lot in return, something immaterial but incredibly rich. At times I almost see three of the students coming alive in my paintings—Vincente Bonacasa, Carlos Turrez and Arturo Boada?! What talented little devils they were!

I regret leaving this behind. Clémence, please visit me when you are next in Paris, it would be a pleasure. I'm at Rue de Ravignan 13.

From your friend,
PICASSO

From Pablo Ruiz y Picasso to Clémence Jacquinet, Barcelona, Monday, 4 April 1904

What are your childhood memories of school? Take time to ask your peers and students to do a free-writing exercise for 30 minutes, in which they recall their school experiences and trajectories. Consider these experiences together and consider how you remember them.

Is one hour a week enough time for an art class?

MY DEAR FRIEND,

Sorry for not replying to you before, but things here are going downhill. Ferrer is having an affair. I can no longer hold it in. I know this is nothing to do with me, but Leopoldine is my friend and this other woman? I hear she is an anarchist and will teach at the Modern School next year. Mary, do you think it would be the right thing to intervene, even in some small way? I am very torn.

Most of my essays are not being approved by Ferrer anymore. He is so stubborn. <u>He cannot see that any school or institution is an authoritarian agency no matter what, and the proof is that these students are being deprived of an education relating to the language and culture of the community they are part of</u> [Catalonia]. 'Let's teach in Esperanto'—Ferrer said the other day!
I firmly believe education should be neutral and not dogmatic in anyway, I thought that was the purpose of this school.
I'm being too hard perhaps.
My friend, I hope you don't take me wrong, but I've been feeling so tired. I think it is time to depart from here.

Yours,
C. JACQUINET

From Clémence Jacquinet to Mary Cassatt
Barcelona, Thursday, 10 May 1906

— Can schools ever be neutral and not dogmatic?

— Which forms of culture, language, life or knowledge are being excluded from your school system? Why? What do you think should be done about this?

DEAR SOLEDAD,

Do not be distressed or uneasy. I worry that my abrupt departure was difficult for you but rest assured, my beloved, my heart remains with you. I will soon return. This place I have come to cannot hold me.

Sabes te quiere de veras tu

FERRER

From Francisco Ferrer Guardia to Soledad Villafranca
Barcelona, Thursday 2 September 1909

What happens when a radical education project is closed? For example, consider that following Ferrer's execution, an international Ferrer movement (also known as the Modern School movement) spread throughout Europe and as far as Brazil and the United States, most notably in the New York and Stelton Modern School.

Are there acknowledged influences of the Modern School in current educational programmes?

A suspended focus: Art School 2014–2020

Stills by Jennie Guy
Content architecture by Peter Maybury
Captions and other text by Jennie Guy and Fiona Gannon

footage
trailing steps
tripping over collisions
honing in
a suspended focus
with careful footing

The following pages reveal a collection of video stills and images from Art School's archive.

Over the years I have been compelled to capture video chronicles that document this project as it unfolds. I see each film as a portrait. The goal is to show each project as it took place in its rawest and most direct form, so that anyone interested in this work can glimpse a trace of these moments for themselves. The only sound in these short films is the voices of students, artists and teachers set alongside the activities and atmospheres produced within the school. There is no background music or conversation to camera.

I followed my camera through classrooms, gym halls, greens and corridors, catching all sorts of moments, moods and interactions as the students encountered the practice of artists in their midst. I witnessed wildness, lethargy, experimentation, self-consciousness, critical thinking, technique, play, pride and wonder.

Alongside images from the videos that I produced are other stills taken from collaborative video works produced by artists and students, as well as images taken by professional photographers to document public-facing events.

While I am incredibly attached to this archive, I have found it challenging to make a selection for this book. The act of distilling the images was handed over to Peter Maybury, who set the rhythm for this section. Following his selection and layout I worked alongside Fiona Gannon to support the image sequences with text.

What you see in the following pages is—to me—the best timeline of the project to date.

100　　Untitled
　　　　The first Art School residency with John Beattie
　　　　and Transition Year students
　　　　Blessington Community College, Co. Wicklow
　　　　September – December 2014

Learning to use a Steadicam rig to produce a moving-image work exploring the school as a set, stage and studio. John introduced the session by showing the students works by William Kentridge.

Exploring lighting conditions with the protagonist of the film during an early stage of the shoot.

Working together to rehearse a tracking shot requiring close collaboration between a crew of students as they traverse the gymnasium.

Following the protagonist as the sequence shifts outside of the school. The final work combined video and stop-motion sequences, and was accompanied by a dynamic ambient soundtrack.

104 **Untitled**
The first Art School residency with Sven Anderson
and Transition Year students
Blessington Community College, Co. Wicklow
September – December 2014

Selecting vinyl LPs sourced at a charity shop in Dublin city. The records were brought in for a workshop in which the students used sandpaper, blades and electrical tape to physically alter the records' surfaces to create new sounds.

(above)
Listening to rhythmic bursts of noise created by the turntables' needles passing over strips of electrical tape on the surface of records. The students layered these sounds as they each took a turn using the equipment.

(below)
Learning about the different speaker components that can be used in sound installations while auditioning sounds from a database of field recordings captured around the world. Sven introduced these forms to the students from examples of sound installations by Max Neuhaus and Christina Kubisch.

Exploring the resonant characteristics of a transducer mounted to a piece of wood as students develop a prototype for a sound installation outside of their school.

The first stage of developing a sound installation located in a passageway outside of the school. Students chose different field recordings and layered them together to develop new sonic textures.

Curator Jennie Guy and art teacher Turlough O'Donnell standing underneath the semi-permanent sound installation. The installation featured slowly evolving layers of sounds chosen by the students, which moved along four boards fitted with transducers mounted to the ceiling overhead.

108　**Playing**
　　　Residency with Elaine Leader and Transition Year students
　　　Blessington Community College, Co. Wicklow
　　　September – December 2015

(inset)
Elaine discussing the role of model-making in prototyping larger installations. The box demonstrates the scale of the models that the students made in order to design larger forms that were installed within their school.

(background)
The students beginning to perforate large sheets of cardboard to be folded into different structures as they translate their models into architectural interventions. Elaine introduced this enquiry concerning architecture, alienation and transformation through references to Jacques Tati's 1967 non-narrative film *Playtime*.

The students who were involved in the residency inviting other students and staff to experience their school environment as mediated by the architectural interventions they had produced during breaktime.

The classroom transforming into a space of production as students translate their concepts from models to full-scale interventions.

Playing
Residency with Sarah Pierce and Transition Year students
Blessington Community College, Co. Wicklow
September – December 2015

Sarah outlining the parameters of a collaborative task, drawing inspiration from Kazimir Malevich's *Black Square*. The students had to paint a black square three metres by three metres in size, using no rulers and working as a team, mostly in silence.

(above)
The students entering the gymnasium during the first part of *The Square*, a one-act play in which they are the writers, producers, actors and audience.

(below)
The students beginning to form the black square on the wall of the gymnasium.

Students performing *The Square*. Sarah introduced this project through Bertolt Brecht's *Lehrstücke*, and worked with the students to develop a series of phrases and gestures that they sequenced to form the play. The play was performed just once, with no audience other than the students and those involved in the workshop. The play was filmed, but was never screened publicly.

116   **Magnetic Fields**
Workshop series with John Beattie and
Fifth Year art students
Scoil Chonglais, Baltinglass, Co. Wicklow
September 2015

Students taking turns handling a DSLR
camera in order to develop a sense
of the consideration that informs the
cinematography of artists' moving-image
works. John presented these exercises
after discussing work by Stan Douglas,
Omar Fast and Samuel Beckett.

John introducing students to the different factors involved in planning, directing and shooting a scene within a moving-image work.

Developing actions and postures on the school grounds as moving-image experiments.

Students arranging and acting within shots for the video, experiencing what it is like to be both behind and in front of the lens.

Magnetic Fields
Workshop series with Michael West and
Second through Fifth Year students
Scoil Chonglais, Baltinglass, Co. Wicklow
September 2015

Michael developing a concept to work with experimental writing formats, discussing descriptive masks and explaining that sometimes it's easier to describe an abandoned orange peel than to describe yourself.

Developing individual written pieces to be read aloud in class. Michael reminded the students that sometimes the interesting thing about writing is reading.

The students presenting written fragments for discussion. The task involved writing one-minute plays with no objects in them.

Magnetic Fields
Workshop series with Sven Anderson and
Second through Fifth Year students
Scoil Chonglais, Baltinglass, Co. Wicklow
September 2015

Sven presenting sound installations
by Zimoun, developing a sense of what
happens when many objects—or people—
create the same sound together with
minor variations.

Recording different sound environments both inside and outside of the school.

Reading together as part of a student-conducted performance, in which students read random excerpts from different books, opening, closing and turning pages on cue.

Recording a performance based on the sounds of handling paper, building up to a moment in which students scrunched and ripped the paper to form a dense, chaotic rhythm.

Other? Other* Other!
Workshop series with Rhona Byrne and
Fourth and Fifth Class students
Gaelscoil de hÍde and Scoil Mhuire
National Schools, Co. Roscommon
September – November 2015

Preparing materials to create forms to be inhabited by many students at once. Rhona's workshops explored proxemics in relation to installation art, site-specific art and wearable sculptures, working through these forms to examine, identify and celebrate otherness by considering how spaces can make us feel more relaxed or more anxious.

Rhona directing the students into configurations in which they can see what it is like to be positioned in different densities, exploring thresholds and personal space.

Experimenting to see how many students can fit within the shared space at any one point in time. The students developed one wearable sculpture for two, and one wearable sculpture for eleven people. Following the workshops, these sculptures were exhibited in Roscommon Arts Centre.

132 **Other? Other* Other!**
Workshop series with Vanessa Donoso López and Fourth and Fifth Class students
Gaelscoil de hÍde and Scoil Mhuire National Schools, Co. Roscommon
September – November 2015

(background)
Preparing raw materials to be pressed into clay to make intricate tiles bearing traces of the students' homes. Vanessa worked from the idea of being a stranger in a new country, where you might search for similarities to your own country, celebrate your difference or sometimes feel homesick.

(inset)
Vanessa discussing the difference between working with handmade clay from the Wicklow mountains and clay that was bought in a store.

Experimenting with different forms to be set in the clay tiles.

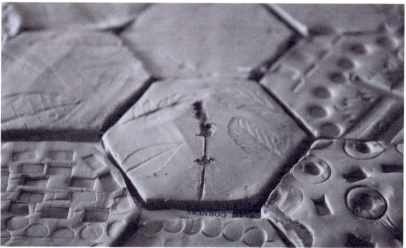

(above)
Building geometric forms alongside the marks of plants and other materials. The hexagonal tiles were derived from Vanessa's introduction to the architecture of Antoni Gaudí, through whom she recalled traces of her own home in Barcelona.

(below)
Developing a form in which tiles produced by different students were brought together to build a collective form titled *The Corridor of Culture*. This delicate, floor-based arrangement was exhibited in the Roscommon Arts Centre following the workshops.

136   **Bead Game**
Residency with Fiona Hallinan and
primary school students
Bray School Project and St Mary's
and St Gerard's National Schools,
Co. Wicklow
March – May 2016

(above)
Preparing to work with casting objects in resin. Fiona's workshop explored working through themes of memory, context and the ephemeral. These workshops were supported by art and philosophy sessions with Katy Fitzpatrick and Aislinn O'Donnell, which explored the relationship between sensation and memory through experiential learning.

(opposite)
Filling moulds with resin and objects selected by the students. The objects embedded in the resin each represented a sound chosen by the student. By resequencing the final resin casts, the students could create different scores that recalled memories of the sounds they had chosen.

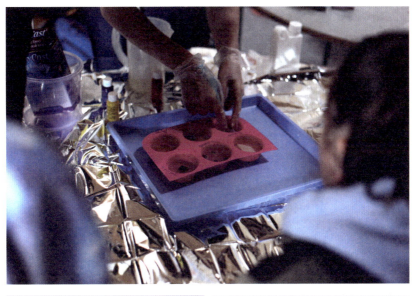

(above)
Laying out the final resin casts to form a score.

(above)
Exploring the woods beside the school in Enniskerry.

(below)
Finding a location within which to arrange the score of resin objects.

Gathering around a scroll of paper on which to place the resin casts. From these cast objects, the students created a collective score of their own and each other's associated sounds.

The Masterplan
Residency with John Beattie and
Ella de Búrca and Fourth, Fifth and
Sixth Class students
D7 Educate Together National School,
Dublin
April – September 2016

(previous spread)
Developing hand gestures for a spoken-word opera. The central motif was an examination of the purpose of school, not only in the past and the present, but also in future societies. The research was framed around a trio of questions: What was school for? What is school for? What will school be for? During the first sessions, John and Ella worked with the students' answers to create a performance in which students conducted each other via hand signals to trigger reading the answers aloud.

(above)
Students rehearsing the spoken-word opera in their classroom. Their school was in the process of being relocated to an area of Grangegorman that was undergoing rapid urban renewal. The residency explored the idea of the masterplan, as a planning device.

(above)
Students, artists and teachers walking to the location where their new school will be built.

(below)
Conducting and performing the spoken-word opera near the site of the new school in Grangegorman.

144   **The Student Body**
Residency with Rhona Byrne and
Transition Year students
Blessington Community College,
Co. Wicklow
September – December 2016

Measuring the dimensions of different
school passages to learn more about
proximity in these spaces. Rhona worked
with students to consider the role of
intimate, personal, social and public
spaces in the school.

Students from Rhona's workshop directing other students around a roundabout that they had created at a central junction in the school, exploring how this new feature altered student traffic during peak times between classes.

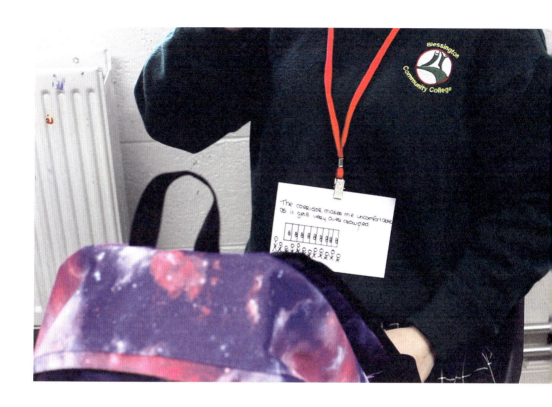

Developing lanyards expressing how the students felt about the different spaces they were exploring in their school. This idea was based on making observations as a user of the school, representing the behaviours of other people and how they were using and experiencing their school environment.

148 **The Student Body**
Residency with Maria McKinney and
Transition Year students
Blessington Community College,
Co. Wicklow
September – December 2016

Students demonstrating in the school halls, carrying placards they developed to make their voices and needs heard by the school.

Maria introducing the students to elements of her practice, developing a focus on the concept of gut flora as a form of brain, and linking this to the idea of 'the student body'. The students explored this concept, shifting from a biological body to a political body.

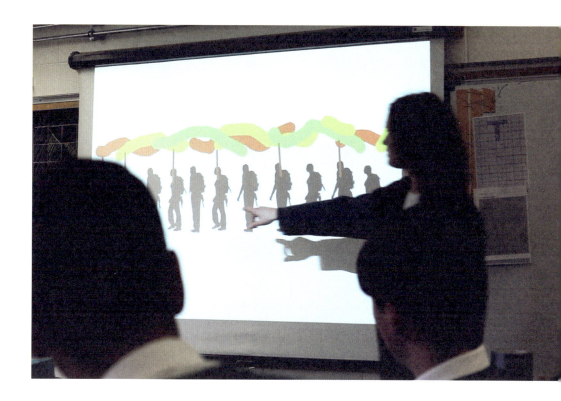

Outlining a potential form for a sculpture that fuses the idea of gut flora and protest, the colourful inflatable shapes based on stomach bacteria, and the students wielding these forms among placards from their protest.

Students carrying the finished sculpture exploring the notion of the student body, enacting a demonstration both inside and outside of the school for other students and staff to witness. The students had devised the route for the protest by drawing a map of their school from memory, devoting attention to specific areas that they could access, and other areas that they could not access.

154

The Masterplan
I'll be in your camp: will you be in mine?
Workshop series with Naomi Sex and
Transition Year students
St Paul's CBS and Technological
University Dublin (TU Dublin)
September – November 2016

(opposite)
Naomi reviewing prints with one of the students. During the workshops she discussed how printmaking has historically played a key role as a powerful and creative tool for artists to get their ideas across to a wide cross-section of society, as it provided them a means of replicating their imagery.

(above)
Gathering around the printing press.

Students working with their art teacher, Danielle Heffernan, to develop plates to make their own prints.

Learning about the safety procedures required in different stages of the printing and etching processes.

Students reviewing different prints by current fine-art students created in the print workshop at TU Dublin. The students' school is just down the road, and this was the first time they had access to this nearby facility.

160   Untitled
        Workshop series with Hannah Fitz
        and primary school students
        Brideswell, Feevagh and Tisrara National
        Schools, Co. Roscommon
        October – December 2016

One of the collaborators demonstrating
their own technique in a gesture of
mutual betterment and generosity.

Hannah's collaborators gazing upon the disastrous display of strength performed by their colleague with mild amusement.

Hannah introducing the students to her sculptural practice.

(opposite above)
A ghost moving through the classroom, although the singular might not actually apply, as a third hand suggests.

(opposite below)
The work produced by the group took shape as a theatrical interaction between various actors, with groups of students performing the role of a table by holding its cloth together, or a window holding its frame on either side and two curtains, or a beam of light by rolling out yellow cloth while the sun was lifted slowly from the other side of the window. Each entity was performed by multiple students.

(below)
The potted plant remains curious,
guarded, distracted and ready.

164 **Untitled**
Workshop series with Jane Fogarty and primary school students
Brideswell, Feevagh and Tisrara National Schools, Co. Roscommon
October – December 2016

The team overseeing a group process making adjustments to a sculptural work. Jane presented ideas about paintings operating as snapshots of a moment in time, while sculptures deal with space and time. They looked at how painting and sculpture can overlap and how time can be represented through both media.

Jane guides her collaborators in finding new forms and compositions in clay and paint. During the workshop, Jane reflected on the passage of time in making, and the time contained in each object.

The group arranges a display of their work. Using fabric and clay, students created a colourful object arranged into a semi-abstract still-life composition. This process operated like a clock, with each object representing twenty minutes of the young artists' time and energy.

An artist holds one of her compositions.

168   **Untitled**
Workshop series with Kevin Gaffney
and primary school students
Brideswell, Feevagh and Tisrara National
Schools, Co. Roscommon
October – December 2016

Kevin introduces the students to his practice, to the worlds of film-making, and to the role of fiction in depicting alternative realities. He showed them an excerpt of his film *A Numbness in the Mouth*, which is in the Irish language, and takes place in an Ireland of the near future, in which the country has become a self-sustaining militarised island where climate change has benefited agricultural production.

Student producers engage in world-building. Throughout the day, Kevin continually referenced how film-making informs content that the students experience frequently, including movies, cartoons, TV shows and music videos. The aim of the workshop was to give students agency to critically evaluate the films and media they consume, and to encourage them to create their own.

A captive audience.

Multiple characters relate in an under-the-sea mermaid world starring Mr Bean and a golden egg.

Art School Chat Show
Hannah Fitz, Jane Fogarty and Kevin Gaffney
Event at Roscommon Arts Centre
December 2016

(below)
Jane and Kevin approaching the audience of students and answering questions.

(opposite)
Kevin and Jane inviting a student on stage for the chat show. The show was staged at the Roscommon Arts Centre, providing a space for the artists and the students to discuss the workshops they had developed over the past months in front of an audience of their peers. The chat show featured screenings of films that documented the workshops, alongside works by Rachel Maclean, Tacita Dean and Sam Taylor-Johnson and a musical interlude by Señor Coconut (Uwe Schmidt).

The artists interviewing their collaborators, asking questions such as: How would you describe the workshop to someone who wasn't there? What was your first reaction to this artwork? Did your opinion of the workshop and the artwork that you made change during the course of the day?

176

How to Swim on Dry Land
Residency with Sarah Browne and Fifth
Year art students
Killinarden Community School, Co. Dublin
October 2016 – March 2017

Stills from the collaborative video produced as part of Sarah's residency. Image courtesy of the artist.

(inset)
A student holding a slab of black glass mimicking an iPhone. Image courtesy of the artist.

Tracing paper being used to frame a music-video version of the pantoum produced as part of *How to Swim on Dry Land*. A pantoum is a verse form that redistributes lines to produce new meanings. Image courtesy of the artist.

One of the students wrapping themselves in an emergency blanket. In the video work, this occurs while the pantoum realigns with the question 'How is the sea formed / For different creatures?' Image courtesy of the artist.

180 **Image of the Self With and Amongst Others**
Residency with Mark O'Kelly and Transition Year students
Our Lady's School Terenure, Dublin
September 2016 – March 2017

Composing a silhouette as the first stage of collectively painting a large-scale group portrait.

Stretching to reach the top of the canvas.

Tracing the first marks of the portrait.

Working together as the figures begin to take form. Mark worked with the students to question the significance of the group portrait in the current age of the selfie. Mark explored this process through references to his own work, Rembrandt's *Night Watch*, Ursula Reuter Christiansen's *Kvinder Trem! / Women Forward* and Marlene Dumas' *The Teacher*.

The final acrylic-on-canvas painting, *Image of the Self With and Amongst Others*, measuring 550 x 250 cm. Meeting over six consecutive weeks, Mark and the students explored the power and the challenges inherent within a group as they worked to reconsider identity forming their collective image, supporting the concept that 'the whole is greater than the sum of its parts'. The painting featured in the group exhibition *It's Very New School* at Rua Red in 2017. Photo credit: Louis Haugh.

186 **The Masterplan**
I'll be in your camp—will you be in mine?
Workshop series with Karl Burke and
Transition Year students
St Paul's CBS and Technological
University Dublin (TU Dublin)
January – April 2017

Discussing Erwin Wurm's *One-Minute Sculpture* series with students before preparing to make their own variations of the work.

Appropriating objects from the classroom to construct temporary sculptures. Karl photographed each sculpture, capturing an inventory of the different forms the students explored.

Transforming rulers into elements of a temporary sculpture.

190

It's Very New School
Exhibition with John Beattie, Sarah Browne, Ella de Búrca, Priscila Fernandes, Mark O'Kelly, Maria McKinney and Sarah Pierce
Curated by Jennie Guy
Rua Red, South Dublin Arts Centre, Tallaght, Co. Dublin
March – April 2017

The Student Body by Maria McKinney runs diagonally through the exhibition space. The school bags prop up a set of posts, each supporting a letter forming the phrase 'the student body' on one side and 'the second brain' on the other. On the right hangs the finished painting by Mark O'Kelly and his collaborators, *Image of the Self With and Amongst Others*.

On the left, Priscila Fernandes' project *A friend in common* displays a series of imagined letters between the Spanish educator and anarchist Francisco Ferrer i Guàrdia and a variety of prominent late nineteenth- and early twentieth-century artists in which the topics of art and education are discussed. Photo credit: Louis Haugh.

Dublin City Council public art manager Ruairí Ó Cuív introducing the exhibition on the opening night. Photo credit: Dave Reilly.

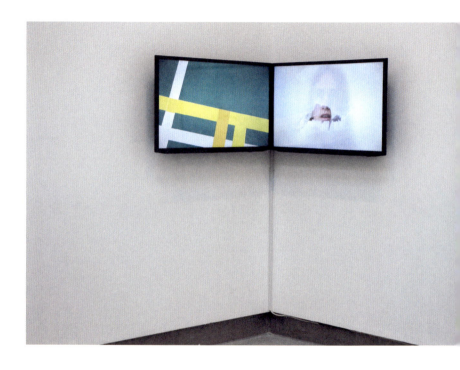

Installation view of *How to Swim on Dry Land*, developed by Sarah Browne and student collaborators. Photo credit: Louis Haugh.

Installation view of Priscila
Fernandes' *A friend in common*.
Photo credit: Louis Haugh.

(opposite)
Sarah Pierce preparing *The Square* with collaborators from Tallaght Community Arts. The performance evolved as 'a roaming set of memorised chants and gestures that speak abstractly to ideas of learning and gathering, and what it means to act, make art and be together' (Sarah Pierce). Photo credit: Dave Reilly.

(above)
Performer from Tallaght Community Arts singing: *Who did this to you?*, a line from the one-act play *The Square*.
Photo credit: Dave Reilly.

Installation view of *The Masterplan* by Ella de Búrca and John Beattie. The spines of the books are labelled with students' responses to questions concerning the purpose of school in the past, the present and in the future. Examples of titles include: *For Men to be Successful in Business*; *For Developing Skills and Interacting With People*; and *For Learning How to Learn*. A row of speakers along the floor form a sound installation that fills the room with the voices of students whispering and chanting these titles in unison. Photo credit: Louis Haugh.

198   **Birds of Prey**
Residency with Maria McKinney and Fourth Class students
St Mary's National School, Maynooth, Co. Kildare
September – December 2017

Maria introducing her residency and its focus on animals, sculpture, ecology and balance within the environment through her own project, *Sire*, also referencing works such as Sarah Pierce's *Birdcalls*, Sean Lynch's *Peregrine Falcons Visit Moyross* and Marcus Coates' *Dawn Chorus*.

(above)
A falconer from Newgrange Falconry and an owl visiting the school in order to activate the sculptural work.

(below)
An owl poised on top of the sculpture—or as part of the sculpture. The perch is composed of all of the students' talons combined into a singular form.

Students fabricating multicoloured talons to be combined in a collective sculptural installation. Maria invited the students to think through her own work with animals, and to contemplate the idea of a sculpture that was only complete when in contact or conjunction with an animal.

A student admiring his new talon prostheses.

202 **I Sing the Body Electric**
Workshop series with Clare Breen,
Maeve Mulrennan and Orlaith Treacy and
primary school students in collaboration
with EVA International
Scoil Ída Naofa (Raheenagh), Mahoonagh
and Ahalin National Schools, Co. Limerick
January – March 2018

[previous spread]
Students devising their own exhibition, guided and led by Orlaith and with the support of Limerick City Gallery of Art, who made their drawing collection available for the task. Orlaith tracked her own progression from being an artist to a curator, also referencing the practices of Group Material and Triple Candie. *I Sing the Body Electric* ran in conversation with EVA International in 2018, bringing elements of its themes to schools in Limerick. The project introduced students to the idea and practice of curation, an area not usually addressed in art education until master's level. Photo credit: Deirdre Power.

[above] Students standing poised with markers, tasked with outlining what comes to mind when thinking of an art gallery. Photo credit: Deirdre Power.

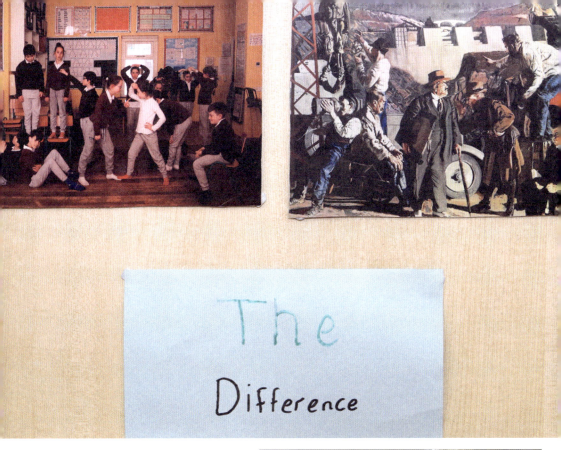

[above]
Clare working with students to re-enact Seán Keating's *Night's Candles are Burnt Out*, painted during the construction of Ardnacrusha hydroelectric power station, which began in 1925. This painting was the impulse for EVA International 2018. Photo credit: Deirdre Power.

[below]
Students working with Maeve to develop three-dimensional constructed objects for The Museum of 6th Class, which looked at the theme of coming-of-age. Students discussed this using nation-building and national identity to segue into personal identity and selfhood at a time of transition. Photo credit: Deirdre Power.

Your Seedling Language
Adam Gibney
Permanent art commission
Curated by Jennie Guy
St Catherine's National School,
Rush, Co. Dublin
June 2019

Your Seedling Language consists of two parts: a cluster of sound-and-light-producing sculptures in the school's entry stairwell, and a sensor tower outside of the school.

The artwork utilises environmental data that is commonly related to the growth of plants. The moisture of the soil, light and temperature outside of the school provide organic compositional parameters that manipulate a generative, eight-channel vocal composition.

With over 1,000 syllabic samples to call upon, the artwork unravels ideas surrounding the theory of biolinguistics, providing the school with a language of its own.

The development of this work stemmed from research into Fingal's rich multicultural history and how this influenced the now unused Fingallian dialect. It celebrates the mixture of cultures and languages that flourish in this school. Image courtesy of the artist.

How many elsewheres?
(For four voices)
Daniela Cascella

I deliberately ask Sven not to send me plenty of documentation of the two residencies: I was not there; some other form of transmission must be set in motion. I am drawn toward the speculative and transformative force of listening from afar, through conversations, and through the imagination: in each instance of embodiment there is a displacement, for every presence a loss, for every sound captured an excess that overflows it. I listen to the few signals I receive from another island, even if sparse, and think with them, write through them: tuning in with attention rather than stating 'I don't have enough', and focusing the attention on the signal rather than the source, on the changing and entangled nature of listening past the demarcation of borders—of culture, of age, of geography and of the mind. Sounds are never complete, sounds are always plenty. They move, prompt thinking, wander. Sounds as they're perceived can enhance a sense of presence, and then they're gone; they may return, perhaps in disguise; they may haunt, or be unheard; and a moment after, they may be revealing, remembering as a child, believing…

… from an island to another, even though borders are closing in I can hear transmissions, from an island to another. Sounds, heard, recorded, passed on and received, discovered, arranged, dismantled and rearranged. Sounds, scraps and fragments, trespassing. I listen between what is recorded and what is not there: to what I thought I could hear, even when not entirely plausible. In the recorded sounds I recollect experiences I never witnessed. That is the precise, mutable, precise, and mutable limitless madness of acoustic memories which disguise themselves among other restless thoughts, in sounds heard as if imagined and then, gliding over the entire classroom, and turning into the classroom, entwined into the floorboards, and through the ceiling into the trees outside. Here's a full sound, stretched right up to the ceiling and outdoors, along the horizon, a sound so tightly laced around the building of the school as if to prevent the walls from falling apart, then expanding, covering the walls like a second skin, or insect wings, hovering above me from a secret structure of sensory perception now made public in this workshop, and the walls are rolling up toward me and increasingly blurred, boundless, and now my thoughts once enclosed are through the sounds, exposed, quickly as if a sudden gust had lifted off a heavy layer of dried leaves. I heard the recordings. Then a long stretch of silence. Then the sounds again, without a form that could be recognised or assigned to a style, a form unheard of and perceived, plausible, dictated by the sounds' own core, mutable and precise, mutable, limitless, doubled or split, split, trapped, trapped in that recording device, attuned sometimes, sometimes out of sync, trapped in echo, becoming place, I am not there, never quite got there, have always been there and have never again been,

in the school.

WE MADE A HOLE IN THE SCHOOL!

        A zone suspended between sky and earth
        Between classroom and outdoors

A place to *be*, not only to be real.

Gordon Matta-Clark. I need to think more about Gordon Matta-Clark. I wonder what these children will perceive, and understand, if any of them carries on studying art and one day will encounter the work of the artist who made holes and crevices in buildings, cut them up, sliced away portions of walls and ceilings, to carve out a zone suspended between sky and earth. 'We did it too. We've been there. But we did it with sounds,' they will know.　　And *to have done it*, not theorised it: to have suffered it, gone through it. Before any conventional discussion of site and non-site, before any concerns around acoustic ecology, before what is allowed and forbidden, no matter what: sound can pierce walls. And minds, and hearts, and ways of being.

　　… I can't even see images. I reconstruct a story from conversations and what is heard, overheard, the story of a child who a long time ago, once upon a time, on an island of the mind, listens to an archive of field recordings, and the more the recorded sounds unravel, the more it seems like they're arising not from an individual source but from an assembly of clashing spirits—heard in sequence for the first time, their variable arrangements give rise to an idea of noise previously unheard of. With the excuse of assembling a document of those sounds, the child began a mental fugue into becoming sound, into becoming place—she did not want to learn of music as notion, but rather wanted to perceive the sounds' commotion, and to understand herself, the classroom, the other children in the classroom, similarly: as commotions. She knew, after listening to those recordings, that the category in which the world presents itself is enchantment: not a word you heard often in a classroom those days. She would find enchantment again on the way home, or in the rooms of an empty school building. Not in the sounds of modern communication: other frequencies were in motion. She knew she was elsewhere.

This is my favourite spot for listening; not the most quiet but I like it here. If you open the windows you can smell grass freshly cut from the lawn, and cool air, and see cobwebs on the walls, ladybirds in the spring. I am thirty-five, but here I am fourteen. I have just entered this vast hall and I begin to hear a different space. I run and run and run around in circles, jump and stamp my feet and they echo and echo and echo, and I still smell the familiar grass and see cobwebs but truly I am in a vast, strange hall built in another country and I am running around in circles in this hall that echoes and echoes and echoes, here and not here and this is happiness, pure happiness.

Breathless, eager and in part puzzled with the coming wonder. A crackling sound, calling for concentration in the impeding bundle of noises. Something intelligible must emerge, no it does not, it must be legible, no it is not, this is noise, a crackle, a tumult. I stop worrying about meaning; I am with these crackles and tumults. Metallic sort of scraping, growing louder and louder, and some of these noises are distinct, but they seem to emanate from a background that is far away, remote, not familiar. Waver, waver, now closer, now farther, now fainter, flatten, collapse, noise, buzz. I could have said a million things, but I said 'I don't know'…

… I don't know. I really don't know what we're being asked to do in this workshop. But these sounds echo and echo and echo, and a short while ago I was in a vast hall built in another country and I was running around in circles in the hall that echoes. It doesn't matter if I don't know: I could hear, I was there in my hearing. For a few minutes this room was also another room. And now that the sound is over and it only looks like a classroom, I see the others slightly differently. I am curious: how many sounds have they heard too, in how many elsewheres have they been? How many other places does each of us hold in hearing, not always perceivable, sometimes concealed? Now I know: that knowing is nothing without perceiving, nothing without spending time, nothing without attending, sensing, failing, trying, hearing, being always here, always elsewhere.

***

Shift the attention from the children to the teachers. To the emotional condition of a teacher sharing a personal engagement with sound-making, listening, recording, surrounded by different waves of enthusiasm, curiosity, scepticism, puzzlement and exhilaration, all at once. Consider how a workshop on sound holds, shakes, questions, reforms very private and very shared dimensions, in ways that are never entirely predictable, or controllable. A group 'trying to keep something afloat,' Sven says to me. At this point I begin to imagine *A Handbook of Maxims for Teaching Sounds*—not a syllabus, not an instruction manual, but a record of impressions. I said I begin to *imagine*; like Sven once wrote to me concerning another of his multilayered, visionary projects, 'there is no physical manual; instead, inhabiting this action becomes the manual'. What would be in the book, inhabiting the actions of teaching and listening, rather than spelling them out according to rules and outcomes?

Nobody ever taught us any of this, formally. We pass on a state of mind; a manner of being and moving in the built environment—of a classroom, a school, a town, a city; of being attentive to sounds that in part grew out of some private encounters with recordings, at a time when the world of music seemed to turn upside down with compositions and improvisations so otherworldly, elusive, and yet their elusiveness drew us, and tempted, puzzled, exhilarated us. The sense of being partially without coordinates while listening, though driven by a core of attention. Time spent listening, not being linear, holds little promise of predictable outcomes, but vital possibilities to develop scrutiny, and for questions to continue and unfold.

If no outcome is defined and declared at the beginning, a singular disposition can be sensed and articulated: exactly because it is not written down.   The curiosity of taking over a public space, in the built environment, by placing audio inside it: sometimes it is important to make a hole in the school.   There's a vitality in what Sven calls 'that swaying between something very close, personal, individual; immediately taken up by the chaos of the group, or even by the imperative to communicate with others about what you are trying to create'.   Working with sounds develops attention and alertness to other forms of finding and transmitting knowledge, that are not limited to the page, and to accepted syntax and consequential reasoning, but expand into the environment, into understanding as entanglement. These other forms, these other sensibilities, must be nurtured and can never be taken for granted: any of us who's presented sound work in the ill-adjusted setting of an academic conference will know this.

Listening can offer ways out of an impasse—aesthetic and non.

Sounds are plural, so we learn to live in the plural.

It takes time, and dedication, to draw in your mind the architecture of the vast hall in which you thought you ran and ran and ran as a child; the experience of having been in the imaginary architecture will stay, it will reawaken in the least expected moments.   We live with estrangement, experiences don't always go somewhere final, and we learn this by listening—an experience that can often be estranging. Listening, that is, an experience which can be often estranging.

To work with listening is to work with the non-conclusive, and the non-concluded: an opening toward understanding which is never dogmatic.   Irreverence, irreverence, irreverence.

Learning to listen is to learn a sense of the spirit of things, places, connections, rather than all-comprehensive transparency. Like the impression left by the telling of a story, in listening we inhabit the elusive and the ephemeral and allow them to shape us as much as the accountable and the tangible. To work with no expectations toward sounds gives form to an exploratory, porous form of understanding that welcomes chance and accidents.

A comprehension of sound can be achieved before any formalised talk of music is introduced. Silence should not be uncomfortable. Now you can spell MARVEL, now you can listen to it. Listening to sounds affords a way of knowing that escapes the explanatory bias of scholarship and the overload of explanation. This does not mean listening is acritical: it tears open the fabric of linearity and patches it with expanded arguments of sensorial and sensuous engagement. We need this.

***

A lightning storm! A new shiver, through a sound I had not quite heard before, not quite entirely, elsewhere of every other. It opens in turn into a new sense of acoustics. Luminous, it changes the classroom into the place where echoes abandon themselves to inertia, visual rhythms of light and sudden jolts of thunder call one another and hybridise, and I no longer know what I am hearing, but continue to be drawn into these signals: what room is this, what space? It is the eruption of an electrified state as a condition of consciousness. And then, when the recording ceases to play, I will move again in a deepened pace and flowing.

[Many years later]
A tone, a noise, an echo: of the same substance as these walls. And then—where to find, within these walls, that longing which gave thought its purpose and its boundless spaces, that feeling of an unknown origin whose sounds marked our lives? What remains now are the tones we

heard in stillness, or in our circling around those school rooms and halls. For some time we thought we'd become those rooms, and a residue of us stayed. Even if it was only dust to be touched again by sounds, then swept away in the corners, even if the sounds were faint, we lingered on, in the site where those recordings were first heard, those sounds that seemed to be committed to us and to us only. Those days with sounds we practised small gestures of attention, and we began to perceive peripheral transformations despite ourselves, the ebb and flow of listening in the atmosphere of a room. Earlier today, trying to recollect some of those sounds, they seemed so obscure; at the time, none of us could integrate them into any notion of understanding, and yet they were not senseless, gratuitous whims. Their place continues to be on the periphery, their area is mutation, not always univocal, not always progressive. Linear was not the task we were given that day; conclusive it was not either. It had to do with attention. With transformation. With imagining that which is not seen or heard—not immediately available, yet present in materialities which demand attunement to be perceived. Remember we were in the room, in the school. I know we'll hear those sounds again later, not quite there and not quite so, in an atmosphere between forms, suspended, enquiring, without dogma and with precision—to become. You must have heard a lot, to no longer want to *express* anything.

38th EVA International: I sing the body electric
Matt Packer

I Sing the Body Electric was a project of classroom-based curatorial workshops directed by Jennie Guy in collaboration with curators Clare Breen, Orlaith Treacy and Maeve Mulrennan and three schools in Co. Limerick. The project was developed as a response to an invitation to contribute to the wider programme of the 38th EVA International (Ireland's Biennial of Contemporary Art, in 2018), where it unpacked some of the biennial's core thematic ideas (power, selfhood and nationalism) and exercised these ideas through group workshops with 10–12-year-olds across schools in Raheenagh, Castlemahon and Ahalin.

This text is not designed to do the job of exhaustively describing and reviewing the project, but it will chart some of the conversation points that were shared between Jennie Guy and myself as the proposal for the project was taking shape. It was in this process of exchange—among many questions, deliberations and compromising pragmatisms—where many of the defining characteristics and ethics of the eventual project took root. This text is therefore a kind of backstory to the project, but perhaps also serves as a commentary to ideas of educational integration within the context of biennial programming more generally.

***

EVA has a long history of educational programming that has been designed to coincide with, support, provide access to and expand upon its 'main' exhibitionary output.[1] As early as the 1980s EVA appointed education coordinators to develop responsive programmes that deliberately sought to engage young people as artists and exhibition-makers (the result was typically an exhibition), which by the end of the decade had developed

---

[1] EVA International is Ireland's Biennial of Contemporary Art based in Limerick. It was established in 1977 and prior to 2012 was an annual exhibition respectively known as 'Exhibition of Visual Art', 'EVA' and 'ev+a'.

into a programme with a communicable identity of its own—'Young EVA'. The basic principle and approach of the Young EVA programme continued for the next three decades, and now boasts an impressive list of artists and arts professionals who cite it as an important influence on their later career and practice.

In 2017, EVA was beginning to reflect on its organisational development and scope out its future for the next five or six years, and it felt necessary to instigate some changes to the programme that would productively dissolve the separation between the exhibition as primary event with the other programmes left to follow in its wake. These were questions of methodology and organisational identity that were also driven by a broader awakening in relation to progressive international arts organisations that recognised that non-exhibitionary programmes were all too often locked in the lower ranks of institutional self-importance— 'relegated to the basement', as Janna Graham has put it, of education programmes in general.[2] As an indicator of communicable values, it is painful to recognise that such programmes tend to find their place in the back pages of the museum or biennial guide, or at the bottom of the e-flux, somewhere in the purgatory between the artistic content, visitor information and the credits. When it does appear (which isn't always the case), it is often detailed without the propositional overtures and authorial styles that characterise exhibition statements, the diagnosis being that education programmes—and schools' programmes particularly—are often limited to being a response to the exhibition that came before them, leaving a few crumbs for educators to collect and return to magic in the classroom.

The better version of the future would seek to move through the phases of educational function that Carmen Mörsch has written of within the context of museum institutions. This would transition from a *reproductive* educational function that endeavours to involve the young

---

[2] Eva Forsman, Nina Suni, Ulla Taipale, Heidy Tiits, Annukka Vähäsöyrinki and Emilio Zamudio, interview with Janna Graham, 'Para-Sites: Following in the Footsteps of Freire', *CuMMA Papers* 12 (2015).

[3] Carmen Mörsch, 'Alliances for Unlearning: On Gallery Education and Institutions of Critique', *Afterall* 26, (Spring 2011).

[4] Inti Guerrero is a Hong Kong-based curator who served as Curator of the 38th EVA International. He is currently Artistic Director of Bellas Artes Projects in the Phillipines

people and uninitiated public within processes of engagement in order to 'ensure the continuation of audiences'; through to a *deconstructive* function that invites participants to 'question, disclose and work on what is taken for granted in art and its institutions, and to develop knowledge that enables them to form their own judgements and become aware of their own position and its conditions'; until finally educational function would be *transformative* 'in the sense of changing society' and art institutionalism itself, by the example of 'shifting the institution in the direction of more justice and less discursive and structural violence'.[3]

Mörsch's structured approach to the function of educational programming offers a road map for radically transforming the organisations and institutions that invite it. In small steps and in our own way, the opportunity of a small pocket of funding from Limerick City and County Council as part of its 'Artists in Schools' programme provided the extra impetus for EVA to exercise a similarly reflexive approach to education within the broader biennial programme.

At the time of initial discussions with Jennie Guy in late 2017, the curatorial framework of the 38th EVA International set by curator Inti Guerrero[4] was in a relatively late stage of development, yet it still lacked some of the descriptive precision that was necessary for public dissemination. This became an unwitting but crucial factor in ensuring that the conversation of developing an educational project within the context of the 38th EVA International was firmly set within the frame of thematic ideas and curatorial articulations, rather than articulated with outfacing statements and public outputs. We saw this as the difference between building an educational project from within a curatorial process and the more common binary task of responding to it after the fact, as education projects are often tasked to do.

Guerrero's curatorial approach to the 38th EVA International was to conceive it less as a monolithic large-scale exhibition, and more as an

and the Estrellita B. Brodsky Adjunct Curator of Latin American Art at Tate, London. See Hatty Nestor, 'Inti Guerrero: "I am trying not to fall into the cultural production and consumption of difference"' at studiointernational.com, 30 April 2018 (accessed 12 May 2020).

5 The referendum to repeal the Eighth Amendment sought to overturn a constitutional act established in 1983 that legally recognised the equal right to life of the pregnant woman and the unborn. The amendment effectively criminalised abortion in almost all

interlocking set of smaller group exhibitions, each circulating their own ideas and points of reference that would at times overlap and at times recede. The then-upcoming referendum in Ireland to repeal the Eighth Amendment[5] (relating to constitutionally enshrined restrictive abortion laws) seemed to haunt all aspects of everyday life in the campaigning that led up to the vote. It also caused many of us in the country to look back at the history of systematic violence against women in Ireland, and look up, down and across to other geographical contexts for better examples and comparative justice. The referendum coincided with and promoted a popular awakening of gender politics internationally,[6] which was reflected in Guerrero's decision to include a presentation and performance by the Artists' Campaign to Repeal the Eighth Amendment, with other works by artists such as Steven Cohen, Roy Dib and Sanja Iveković,[7] whose entire practices have been defined by challenging the intersection of sexual identity, gender and national institutionalism in the respective contexts of South Africa, the Middle East and Eastern Europe.

Another thematic loop in the 38th EVA International was electricity as a metaphor of modernism and infrastructural power, with works such as Uchechukwu James-Iroha's *Power and Powers* (2012) series of black-and-white photographs that depict groups of men elaborately posing with electrical infrastructure in Nigeria; or in the example of Adrian Duncan and Feargal Ward's film installation *The Soil Became Scandinavian* (2018), which recounts the history of sourcing electrical poles from the remote forests of Finland in order to fulfil the Irish government's plans to bring electrification to rural Ireland in the mid-twentieth century. Nationalism itself was present also, amplified by the background noise of President Trump's Twitter proclamations[8] and the death rattle of Brexit,[9] as well as the more positively marketed centenary celebrations of the Easter Rising here in Ireland.[10] It was the evident subject of John Duncan's photographs of Loyalist bonfire constructions in Belfast, and among other works

instances, unless the pregnancy was life-threatening to the pregnant mother. Following a bitter campaign, the amendment was repealed by 66.4% of the voting public.

6   The year 2018 was rocked with disclosures of sexual harassment by leading figures in mainstream TV, film and politics, with many of the accusers empowered by the success of the #MeToo movement in 'calling out' systematic sexualisation and abuses of power.

7   Works included at the 38th EVA International included: Artists' Campaign to Repeal the Eighth Amendment's *Repeal!* (2018)—a procession through the streets of Limerick on

including Ian Wieczorek's delicate paintings of figures held in permanent stasis as they appear to cross boundary fences that the artist renders invisible. It was the issue of nationalism that also led to the decision to avoid the use of a title identity for that year's edition of the biennial, with the idea that the simple title of '38th International' would reinforce the significance of internationalism at a time when it was no longer possible to take it for granted as a universally positive and aspirational notion. It was an interesting reversal of identities when, into this void of a title for the 38th EVA International, Jennie Guy put forward the title of *I Sing the Body Electric*, which was borrowed directly from a Walt Whitman poem.[11]

While the 38th EVA International spun in many different thematics and captured a diverse range of geopolitical references, there was one work that seemed to be a compass point for it all: Seán Keating's *Night's Candles Are Burnt Out* (1928–9), painted while the artist was on self-imposed residency at the site of the Ardnacrusha Hydroelectric Plant in Co. Clare.[12] The painting, almost miraculously, held together the biennial's thematic pathways (gendered institutionalism, electricity, modernism, nationalism and internationalism) within one allegorical frame.

Keating's painting depicts a cast of characters drawn from the range of early twentieth-century Irish society, set in a form of tableau in front of the construction site of what was then the largest infrastructural investment project of the newly independent Irish state. We see a young mother, a child in her arms, with an arm outstretched at the distant horizon, in a pose that is notably more hopeful than the cowering and buckled-over other characters who share the scene. There's a drunken worker, a priest reading a book in ignorance of all around him and a soldier whispering into the ear of an industrialist. *Night's Candles Are Burnt Out* is the most well-known and complete work from an entire series of paintings and sketches that Keating produced of the Ardnacrusha Hydroelectric

---

13 April 2018; Steven Cohen's *Chandelier* (2001–2)—a documented performance of the artist wearing a chandelier, walking through an impoverished homeless district in Johannesburg; Roy Dib's *Mondial 2010* (2014)—a video that charts the road trip of a Lebanese gay couple through Ramallah in Palestine; Sanja Ivekovic's *Lady Rosa of Luxemburg* (2001)—a sculptural replica of a World War I monument re-proposed by the artist with a pregnant figure and named in honour of the political activist Rosa Luxemburg.

Plant while it was under construction. He was evidently fascinated by the project and its impact on Irish society as a whole, optimistic of Ireland's future especially now that it was free from the shackles of its British coloniser, while also aware that such a future would create new winners and new losers that would continue to echo in the decades to come.

The development of the *I Sing the Body Electric* project could not assume a knowledge of Seán Keating and its historic capsulation among 10–12-year-olds, nor could it be assumed that the same students would have any familiarity with EVA or the general form of curatorial practice that seeks to bring different ideas and artworks together in alignment. These deliberations contributed to the focus of the project on curating and the role of the curator in using artwork to tell stories, make arguments and ultimately to bring into relationship a particular kind of world view that could stand up as a proposition against others.

The workshops also brought these students into direct engagement with three Irish curators who led a number of curatorial exercises with them. In one of the workshops devised by Clare Breen at Raheenagh National School, *Night's Candles Are Burnt Out* was performatively re-enacted in the classroom through a discussion of social allegory of the painting, imagined as if that same allegory was to be updated from today's perspective. What new social roles have come to replace the priest, the industrialist and the soldier in the twenty-first century? What major event hangs society in the balance, just as Ardnacrusha was seen to do almost one hundred years ago? In Orlaith Treacy's workshops with Ahalin National School, original works from the Limerick City Gallery of Art were loaned to the classroom as an element of a larger classroom-based exhibition that involved students bringing in domestic objects—from tins of tuna to remote controls—that were organised in thematic and associative relationships. With pupils at Mahoonagh National School in Castlemahon, Maeve Mulrennan used the original historical speculation

---

8 For a general commentary on Donald Trump's use of Twitter see: Amanda Hess, 'Trump, Twitter and the art of his deal', *New York Times*, 15 January 2017. Available at nytimes.com (accessed 12 May 2020).

9 In June 2016, the United Kingdom voted to withdraw its membership of the European Union. 'Brexit' became the common term to describe this withdrawal. For a general overview of Brexit, see Wikipedia.

10 The centenary of the Easter Rising took place in April 2016 to mark the armed

of Keating's painting to create a similar moment of speculation set in the lives of the students, who curated an exhibition of their own photographs capturing their lives at a point of personal transition.

As many of the books published in recent years about curating and curatorial education will confirm and yet do not quite acknowledge, curating—as a subject of practice—is stuck in being a definitively postgraduate affair. The primary school classroom and curriculum remains unacquainted with curatorial thought. Through the project *I Sing the Body Electric*, we got a glimpse of the possibility that a basic awareness of curating at a primary educational level might be an important step towards devolving the institutional authority that still imposes on and intimidates the general public appetite for contemporary art; turning the decisions made by arts institutions and appointed curators into visible structures that anyone can inhabit with their own ideas and responses. Understanding this also represents a form of empowerment; it holds open the idea that art can be a junction box of signs, references and relations without necessarily requiring the skills that are traditionally associated with artistic authorship. If you can't draw the face of Justin Bieber, a shell or a horse, then curating can be a way of juggling all of these things together, with a creative and critical articulacy that can be uniquely your own.

---

insurrection of Irish Republicans seeking to end British rule in Ireland; 485 people were killed in the conflict. It is commonly regarded as the pivotal action that paved the way for Irish independence, which was finally legislated with the Anglo-Irish Treaty in 1922.

11 'I Sing the Body Electric' is a poem that appeared in Walt Whitman's 1855 collection *Leaves of Grass*. The poem is essentially an ode to the physical and spiritual energies of the human body. For further information, see theguardian.com, Books, Carol Rumens' Poem of the Week, 27 July 2015 (accessed 12 May 2020).

12 Seán Keating (1889–1977) produced a number of paintings and sketches during the construction of the Ardnacrusha Hydroelectric Plant in County Clare. At the time, it was the largest project of the newly independent Irish state, and for Keating it represented the promise of a country that was now free to choose its future following the break from British rule. *Night's Candles Are Burnt Out* (1928–9) is the most finished of all works produced during this period, both stylistically and in terms of its allegorical statement. The painting (along with many other works produced during the Ardnacrusha construction) is in the ESB (Electricity Supply Board) collection.

Play like coyote
Alissa Kleist

Unapologetically layered, Kevin Gaffney's films, such as *Far from the reach of the sun* (2018), *A Numbness in the Mouth* (2016) and *The mirror is dark and inky* (2015), provide glimpses into the lives, thoughts, dreams, fears, desires and realities of characters that narrate diverse individual and collective human experiences. *Far from the reach of the sun* depicts a future in which a government-sanctioned drug can alter its users' sexuality, offering a commercialised experience of 'other' and commenting on a legacy of church, state and medical interference in the lives of LGBT/queer people. In the Ireland imagined in *A Numbness in the Mouth*, climate change has benefited agricultural production and citizens are ordered to consume surplus flour to balance the country's supply with demand. The characters in the film respond to this material imposition on their bodies in unexpected, dreamlike ways. *The mirror is dark and inky* juxtaposes images of daily life in Iran with the surreal concerns of a woman whose bathtub is inhabited by a whale.

These works aggregate the personal, social, political, local and universal, denying the totality of fully understanding or representing that which is other and thereby allowing differences and inconclusions to coexist. They position language as an access point to interior worlds and a departure point from which to begin exploring unknown realities. Gaffney has produced work with participants in countries such as Iran, South Korea and Taiwan. Narrated in the native tongues—such as Korean, Farsi, Irish, Mandarin—of the places where they are filmed, his works consider what it means to exist in duality: human and animal, protagonist and subject, separate and together, dissolving and solidifying from one into the other. In his works, we meet the artist, ourselves and others, and encounter a social heteroglossia that does not produce a whole and yet flourishes in its own polyvocality.

Gaffney was part of a trio of artists selected to deliver workshops in three small, rural primary schools in Co. Roscommon.[1] Over a period of two days in September 2016, he introduced groups of 10–12-year-old students to film-making processes, and discussed the conception of ideas, their visualisation and realisation. He invited students to share this activity with fellow classmates by working together as a crew and presenting their film ideas to their peers. The introduction included the artist's description of his own approach to film-making and his motive for creating moving-image works that explore how identity is formed and performed.

Gaffney began to create personas and plotlines he could relate to in response to the stereotypical characters and repetitive storylines in mainstream film and television programmes. His films question and disrupt normative or established aesthetic, social, political and geographical orders to portray alternative realities where characters become vehicles for personal and societal subconscious desires and struggles. During his workshops, Gaffney encouraged the students to begin to treat film as a speculative, rather than affirmative, mechanism to critically interrogate their external environments, while also offering the potential to navigate personal narratives. Established clichés and genres were questioned through a group dialogue and the screening of some of the artist's films—works that do not necessarily offer dénouement/'unknotting', the conclusive stage at the end of a film, when the plotline is explained.

Following Gaffney's initial introduction, the students were invited to form groups of five and to generate a shared story through participating in an adapted version of *Exquisite Corpse*, the Surrealist parlour game.[2] The groups were asked to write down, unseen by their neighbours, either an idea, a location, a character, a second character or a genre on a section of a folded sheet of paper which, when unfolded, formed the starting

---

1 The three schools were Tisrara, Brideswell and Feevagh National Schools.
2 The title *Exquisite Corpse* is derived from the French *Le cadavre exquis* ('The exquisite corpse')—a sequence of words that the Surrealist poet and screenwriter Jacques Prévert wrote late one night in 1925. A sentence was composed on the next turn of the game by another player with the addition of *boira le vin nouveau* ('will drink the new wine').

point for a collective plotline that included the personal interests of each student.

Exquisite Corpse is an accessible and simple exercise that by its very nature incorporates a dialogic process in order to produce complex results. The game engenders a collective endeavour that deconstructs grand narratives by replacing them with the fragmented, uncomfortable and often delightfully absurdist summary of individual heterogeneous subconscious musings. In the words of Surrealist artist Simone Kahn, who experienced the game when it was first played, *Exquisite Corpse* offered contributors of all ability 'the possibility of creation and thereby opened, permanently, a door to the unknown'.[3]

The students scripted their films using the characters, ideas, locations and genres generated by the exercise to influence new dialogues and storylines. Their imaginative fantasies procured plotlines that included mind-controlling professor babies and dead squids. Cats undertake quests during World War III. The character of Mr Bean finds a golden egg at the beach that hatches into a mermaid in his bathtub. The groups visualised their film concepts in storyboard form and verbalised them to the rest of the class by acting out narratives in handmade collaged sets and through basic collective gestures, presented with the giddy, energetic, at times hesitant intensity of engaged young participants working in cooperation. Engaged but without a clear end-point or grand narrative, they created a many-legged beast, playfully let loose.

Animals repeatedly appeared as characters in the storylines created by the students during this workshop. They also occur in storytelling and the oral traditions of many peoples, acting as universal symbols in a shared language that can be widely understood. In the Western tradition, fictional events that include animals often teach morality, providing cautionary tales that warn of danger, weakness and

---

[3] Simone Kahn, 'The Exquisite Corpses', in *Surrealist Women: An International Anthology*, ed. Penelope Rosemont (Austin: University of Texas Press, 1998), 19.

other human failings, or speak of how humans and animals are dissimilar. In non-Western storytelling, such as in the tribal folklore of indigenous people of North America, 'animal' characters such as Coyote are allowed to be inexplicable. Coyote is a protagonist, teacher and storyteller full of contradictions. He is an animal and a demigod, a saviour of mankind and a trickster, a powerful hero and a lustful fool. In some stories, he takes the form of a raven, a crow, a hare and a bear. In West African mythology, he is Ashanti, a spider. Jung describes him as 'God, man and animal at once… both subhuman and superhuman, a bestial and divine being',[4] a polysemous creature allowed to transgress human expectations.

The animals in Gaffney's films act as shared metaphors, rather than symbols, for exploring other ways of existing. They are not anthropomorphised but complicate the reading of human narrators and their worlds. References to birds, spiders, whales, mosquitoes, worms, cockroaches, fish and rats allow us to imagine the transition from one being to another, of being through the bodies of other beings. Our planet, affected by climate change and an alarming loss of biodiversity, could undeniably benefit from equipping more people to imagine future narratives from a non-human perspective.

Art School demonstrates how artists can become complex characters: teachers and experts, antagonists and authorised rule breakers. Coyotes of sorts. By making accessible, but not resolving, complex processes—in Kevin's case, to deconstruct how films are constructed—while encouraging play and experimentation, artists can create 'mess', something that is avoided within traditional classrooms but which they are skilled at managing. During Kevin's Art School workshop, the traditional construct of a story arc or narrative was skewed in favour of a Surrealist exercise, the finished 'product' becoming a collection of non-linear subjects contributed by a collective trying to make sense of the absurd.

---

[4] Barry Holstun Lopez, *Giving Birth to Thunder, Sleeping with His Daughter: Coyote Builds North America* (New York: Avon Books, 1977), xviii.

The workshops delivered in Roscommon alongside Gaffney's were presented by artists Hannah Fitz and Jane Fogarty. Fogarty, whose practice examines painting and its ontology, explored where the acts of painting and sculpture overlap, and how they can create a visual representation of time. Students she worked with constructed freely assembled one-minute clay sculptures. Energetic making was punctuated by structured moments of reflection as the group considered the concrete representations of five minutes of making. They formed textured, multilayered structures accented in paint and tacitly engaged in a process that tangibly captured a moment of time. The sculptures created during this session became the still-life objects for the next. The group painted them from multiple perspectives on sheets of cardboard. Fingers replaced brushes, and the analytical act of still-life painting dissolved into a collective act of sculptural installation, as the cardboard paintings were slotted together and assembled into tall, free-standing sculptures. The workshop enabled the group to learn about form, balance and composition, while not attempting to visually resolve abstruse, intangible concepts. Fogarty's approach to teaching was playful and light rather than didactic, while not denying participants an open-ended experience of complexity.

Hannah Fitz's sculptural works embody the agency and performativity of objects, and the participants in her workshop were invited to use their own bodies and props to make sculptural objects that 'act' like themselves and amplify their 'thingness'. The group filmed themselves struggling to lift a papier-mâché barbell weight to practise how objective reality can be collaboratively constructed and performed. In the temporary alternative world of artist-as-Coyote, normative order slackened. The heavy was light, adults were jesters, and things could temporarily be what you needed them to be, but only through collective conviction and belief. Supported and directed by Fitz, the students created tableaux in which a series of interactions between object-protagonists such as a potted plant, a sunlit window, a table and a ghost were acted out, lending agency to inanimate actors. Colourful handmade props—when combined—formed the foundations of a rudimentary living room: students holding cardboard painted curtains, a window, a yellow ball, green leaves and a blue pot. They came together to undertake the joint re-enactment of intangible everyday occurrences, like sunlight stretching across a room, plant leaves rustling in a sudden soft breeze, a glass of water picked up from a table slowly spilling. Like the conductor of a strange orchestra, Fitz whispered instructions that provided enough cohesion and support to allow the group to begin to master their props and embody the object-actors, cooperatively telling their stories. Together, they existed in the suspended liminality between reality and fiction, exposing the 'joints' of the performance while simultaneously creating footholds for a polyvocal imagining.

Cooperation is defined as the action or process of working together to the same end. The sociologist and author Richard Sennett describes it as something that is inherent in human development and starts from infancy. As human beings grow and develop, we progress from an instinctive cooperation—working with others in order to attain (and obtain) that which we cannot do (or make) ourselves—to a much more multilayered cooperation: from collaborating with peers and allies to working with strangers, antagonists or 'others' who are different to us, whom we don't like, or with whom we actively disagree. He states that cooperation is therefore a skill and craft that needs to be learned and developed. Sennett states that this 'craftsmanship' is not being taught or honed sufficiently, resulting in the contemporary crisis in cooperation evident in our current social, economic and political spheres.[5]

Art does not necessarily change how an individual sees the world, but it can impact on how a person interprets and thinks about it. The three

---

[5] Current responses to events such as Brexit (the withdrawal of the United Kingdom from the European Union following the referendum held on 23 June 2016); the wall that president Donald Trump has threatened to build between Mexico and the US; and growing nationalism in countries such as Greece, Austria, Hungary and Italy in response to the European migrant crisis emphasise global uncooperative societies' growing need for barriers that safeguard against encounters with 'others'.

workshops delivered in Roscommon were characterised by a playful disregard for 'the rules' and established new ways of looking, thinking and working. The workshop outputs were documented and presented during a public moment at Roscommon Arts Centre in December 2016, which was supported by Roscommon curator-in-residence Linda Shevlin. Working with Art School curator Jennie Guy, the artists chose a TV chat show format, compèred by the artists themselves, to show examples of exemplary artists' moving-image works, premiere the films made during the workshops, and host a Q&A session with the pupils about their experience. This event marked the first time that the school groups were able to meet in the same space and view the work produced during all the workshops. The artists screened a series of moving-image works by artists Sam Taylor-Johnson, Rachel Maclean and Tacita Dean that provided an additional context for their own practices and demonstrated how the traditions of film-making, sculpture and painting are represented and questioned by contemporary practitioners. Teachers were sent a list of rehearsal questions in advance of the event to help prepare the students to participate in the chat show. The event subverted the established talk show format and reversed roles: hosts were interviewed by their guests and thereby the 'teachers' became publicly answerable to their students. During the public event pupils from the participating schools got up on stage to answer questions from and pose questions to their hosts. The artists were asked to describe what their daily jobs entail and what it is like to work and live as a professional artist.

The workshops in Roscommon acknowledged the multiple skills that artists possess, while nurturing relationships and safeguarding and holding curatorial 'spaces' in which the artists could develop creatively and professionally. They were supported by an experienced curator, teaching staff and a team of dedicated assistants, and the workshops resulted in new opportunities for the artists, addressing the important question asked by the pupils: how do artists make a living? For Gaffney, the Art School workshops led to additional work at Marino College, a secondary school and further education college in Dublin, where he shared his experiences of working in an educational setting with trainee teachers and staff and influenced their understanding of the value of artists in classrooms.

The workshops designed by Hannah Fitz, Jane Fogarty and Kevin Gaffney offered a pedagogical framework in which alternative types of cooperative learning spaces were created within an existing system that inevitably prepares young people for a market in which individuals are responsible for their successes and failures. They dislodged the master/student dialectic—an exchange that ends in a form of closure—and replaced it with a more inconclusive interaction that does not necessarily seek resolution, common ground or a different kind of interrelationship, but rather 'hears what is not being said'[6] and re-terms 'failure' as 'learning'.

Artists in educational settings promote the teaching of listening, communicating, accepting, questioning and mediating: important 'soft' skills that equip young people to work with and alongside each other. They can help students to negotiate difference and experience a globalising world through the eyes of an 'other', experiences that may foster the type of social cooperation that could help us through our present-day crises. They make the familiar strange and, crucially, they authorise an increasingly rare, slightly wild, open-ended inconclusivity—they let us play like Coyote.

---

6   Richard Sennett, 'The Architecture of Cooperation', lecture, Harvard University, 2012. Listen on YouTube, 19:00–26:00 (accessed 12 May 2020).

Exercising study
Sjoerd Westbroek

Monday. Proposition 1:
'Try to stand that little bit closer to things and people than you normally would.'

Today, when I arrived at the studio, *Failure* was awaiting me—a collection of texts published by Whitechapel Gallery, exploring ways in which art can defy the coercive logic of notions such as success, competence and certainty. I browsed through it randomly, until a text discussing Bas Jan Ader's work written by Tacita Dean[1] caught my eye. It starts with a quote from the ancient story of Icarus, who fell down from the sky when he couldn't control his ambition to fly and the sun melted the wax in his wings. He had come too close to that which fuelled his desires. Practising the proposition above, this overly moralistic tale involuntarily stayed with me, and I more or less stuck to my daily routine, changing it only ever so slightly. Walking towards the nearby park, my arm brushed the walls lining the streets leading up to it—an occasional bicycle forcing me to move sideways. From the park I decided to walk to the airport, which takes about ten minutes. As I entered the terminal, I felt like a stranger, not a traveller, wandering about rather than waiting for a departing flight or perhaps a person to arrive. The airport activated a type of scripted behaviour that I obviously couldn't perform. However, it also felt senseless to challenge the politics around the impossibility to move about freely. My random encounter with the story of Icarus was a bad omen anyway, so I was glad I didn't have to board an airplane, and on my way out I gave a friendly nod to the security person. I walked back to the studio, again seeking closeness to edges and walls, again practising the move sideways. The exercise brought negotiating a newly found proximity to mundane things back to a bodily level.

---

1 Tacita Dean, 'And He Fell into the Sea', in *Failure*, ed. Lisa Le Feuvre (London/Cambridge, MA: Whitechapel Gallery/MIT Press, 2010), 129–30.

***

'I want to study, I do not want to learn.' I am on a busy commuter train, as this remarkable statement by one of the guys sitting in front of me finally makes me give up my attempts to mind my own business. They discuss the differences between master's programmes for which they're considering applying. Comparing several universities, he seems to suggest his choice is guided by a desire to properly engage with study materials, not just to reproduce their content. In my hand I happen to hold a copy of Stefano Harney and Fred Moten's *The Undercommons*.[2] It's actually the second time I'm reading it, and it makes me realise how sometimes you have to be ready to receive the gift of an author. Or, reversely, how I clearly had not yet developed what was needed in order to receive this gift the last time I read it. I cannot claim to understand the book in its entirety, but its notions have been travelling with me for over a week now, and allow me to understand differently these words that casually fly by. Why do we talk so much about learning and so little about studying?

A small quantitative enquiry proves the importance of 'study' for Harney and Moten. In *The Undercommons*, they use the word 'learn' eleven times, including all conjugations. This contrasts poorly to the 138 times 'study' appears. Any attempt to summarise what study entails for them necessarily starts somewhere in the middle, just as study itself. To study is to engage in a situation, which is by definition social, as it means tuning in to the type of activities that are always already going on. Study is what happens before the teacher issues the call to order that clears a space for teaching. It is more akin to the rehearsal of a band, which for Harney and Moten exemplifies a form of intellectuality that arises out of a shared commitment to be together and practise something: a song, an idea, a work. The almost complete absence of learning from *The Undercommons*, a book which, to a large extent, came out of the authors' engagement

---

[2] *The Undercommons* is a work of radical educational praxis in the form of a book, written by poet and scholar Fred Moten and theorist Stefano Harney and first published in 2013.

with the university, speaks volumes. 'But the student has a habit, a bad habit. She studies. She studies but she does not learn. If she learned they could measure her progress, establish her attributes, give her credit.'[3] I take this to mean that, for the authors, the notion of learning has been fully instrumentalised by policymakers and education professionals, who identify observable outcomes that can be measured. I've observed art educators adopting the language of so-called twenty-first-century skills, evolving around notions such as creativity and problem-solving. In that view, art education not only teaches art, but also contributes to learning creative thinking, preparing the student to become the laterally thinking professional society supposedly needs. I am not sure whether art educators should follow this road, as it privileges an essentially economic perspective on the domain of art education, rather than celebrating the messy multiplicity of views as a strength. Therefore, I think Moten and Harney are right in their judgement that any linear notion of this attribute-oriented approach to assessing a student (creativity, learning, progress, etc.) is problematic. It reduces education to the reproduction of a system that has no real interest in stimulating students to articulate study goals that fall outside of the scope of a supposed economic purpose. It is repressive in discouraging study, and not giving space to students to address the issues that are at stake in their lives.

Perhaps learning is still useful as a psychological concept, because in essence it means going through a transformation. To put it even more simply: to learn means to practise personal change. However, it would be interesting to keep learning out of educational discourse, because defining learning outcomes, by definition, adds a normative, perhaps even a coercive framing. Institutionalised education tends to specify what this change must entail. Alternatively, Harney and Moten seem to suggest that education should be about creating space to study. It is up to the community of students and teachers to articulate both the

---

3 Stefano Harney and Fred Moten, *The Undercommons: Fugitive Planning and Black Study* (Brooklyn, NY: Minor Compositions/Autonomedia, 2013), 62.

urgencies and the methods employed to instigate and facilitate this—'study as something not where everybody dissolves into the student, but where people sort of take turns doing things for each other or for the others, and where you allow yourself to be possessed by others as they do something'.[4] I wonder if my commuting student and his friends understand the fact that, by musing on the choices and challenges they face in their lives, study has already started.

***

This text is the result of an invitation by curator Jennie Guy to write about the projects that Rhona Byrne and Elaine Leader have developed as part of the Art School programme. My first encounter with the work they did was through online documentation,[5] which showed the continuity between their artistic practice and what they do with students. Both artists are interested in exploring in-between states and spaces, preferring to work with things that are in movement rather than static. In Elaine Leader's installations the movement of the viewer might trigger a wall to move, up to the point where it almost hits them. While I watch the YouTube clip documenting one of these works, I can feel a bit of its effect on my own body. It somehow brings back a memory of the experience of being in Bruce Nauman's *Green Light Corridor* (1970) a few years ago in an exhibition in London's Hayward Gallery.[6] Lit by bright green fluorescent light, the corridor is so tight it gives a pressing proximity to a wall, an architectural element in galleries more commonly found to carry works rather than impose its presence onto the viewer. Leader's installations also feature architectural models, which seem to invite a more cerebral exploration of how expectations around the function and uses of space can be challenged or undone. She brought this method of moving between different architectural scales to Blessington Community College, working

---

[4] Harney and Moten, *The Undercommons*, 109.
[5] See jennieguy.com, Projects, Art School (accessed 12 May 2020).
[6] The exhibition *Move: Choreographing You – Art and Dance since the 1960s* took place between October 2010 and January 2011 at Hayward Gallery, Southbank Centre, London. It featured works by practitioners in the field of art and dance who use installation to directly influence the movement of the visitor.

with students towards developing large-scale interventions in their school, challenging the habitual uses of its architecture. The students were introduced to Jacques Tati's *Playtime*,[7] and discussed the portrayal of the uniformity of the modernist city, as well as its playful disturbance, in the second half of the film. Following this collective exploration of a formal approach to cinema—studying a formality that expresses a conceptual interest—the students built cardboard structures to alter or disturb these again. The programme suggests a shift from the rigidity of order to a more chaotic, perhaps more human state of affairs.

Rhona Byrne's work also subverts that which gives spatial solidity and longevity to the built environment. Working with materials such as fabric, she designs installations for people to be in together. Space becomes wearable, rendering it mouldable by the sociality it seeks to establish. Interestingly, the exhibition where I first saw a corridor piece by Bruce Nauman was also my first encounter with the work of Franz Erhard Walther, which Rhona's work reminds me of. I vividly remember having one end of *Körpergewichte*,[8] a five-metre-long strap, around my waist, with a friend on the opposite end, while we were leaning backwards and trying to let go. Only mutual trust would allow us to stay in balance without too much physical effort. I read that Rhona is interested in gaps—tensions perhaps—between private thought and public behaviour. To me the works seem to stimulate a heightened awareness of both, by an ever so slight displacement of the habits of mind and body that constitute the very in–outside binary—perhaps even rendering this binary a bit unstable. In the Art School project *Other? Other* Other!* Rhona used the threshold as a conceptual vehicle to encourage the students of Gaelscoil de hÍde and Scoil Mhuire in Roscommon to temporarily linger in this state of transition, by focusing on how a person moves from one space to another, be it an architectural, personal or social space. In her longer residency in Blessington Community College, she designed a series of

---

7   The film *Playtime* by French director Jacques Tati premiered in 1967 and explores the possibility of spontaneous expressions of humanity in a fictionalised modernist incarnation of Paris.
8   Franz Erhard Walther's *Körpergewichte (Nr 48, 1. Werksatz)* is a work from 1969.

exercises that allowed the students to map behaviour within the physical space of the school and intervene in the habitual movements of its users. Students with arrows attached to their backs formed a living roundabout in a hallway, forcing others into a circular movement around them. Back in the classroom, they were guided in articulating their perceptions of the space, how it encourages or discourages social behaviour, which elements are kept out of sight, where do more private experiences happen? Small drawings and notes of these observations are attached to lanyards and worn for a full day to trigger responses from others, potentially creating the possibility for a conversation about these questions. Perhaps this gesture of wearing an observation already nicely demonstrates how a threshold can be used pedagogically, by giving students control over what remains private and what they choose to communicate.

***

Looking at the documentation of Elaine and Rhona's work, the notions they address merge with my own experiences and preoccupations as an artist involved in teacher training at an art academy. What I observe resonates with certain questions I have—which, of course, is not to say that the work deals with the same things I deal with. Perhaps affinity travels more easily than actual understanding. However, to start with affinity is fine, because 'it's exciting for me when we get to that point where the text is open enough that instead of being studied, it actually becomes the occasion of study'.[9] Like text, like artwork. Rhona's emphasis on the tension between private thought and public behaviour makes me wonder whether we actually pay enough attention to the necessity to cultivate both. The question of whether current forms of institutionalised education offer enough space for experiencing things privately before they are made public is especially relevant in this

---

9 Harney and Moten, *The Undercommons*, 109.

context, I think. A school is a kind of liminal space, somehow facilitating the transition between private and public life along various axes. Rhona's students wearing their observations nicely marks such a movement that is temporarily suspended, allowing a school community to go back to some fundamental questions concerning its functioning. To get at that point, a question is posed that serves not as a learning outcome, but as an occasion for study. The gesture of wearing one's thoughts also marks the possibility to bring something new into the world. Perhaps it is an exemplary preparation for what Hannah Arendt conceptualised as an action:[10] the performance of the new, witnessed by a group of persons who are equals, precisely in how they differ from each other. From this perspective, the space of action, the enactment of the new, is the only true political domain. However, before there is any such appearance, there is thinking, there is learning, there is seclusion. Perhaps the secret is the critical other of the sociality that education typically seeks to encourage.

I have worked in several educational spaces that have been remodelled following the paradigm of transparency. For instance, the canteen of the art academy where I teach is transformed into a publicly accessible restaurant, as an interface between the school and the 'real world'. Another common practice, at least in the Netherlands, is removing walls between classrooms to create co-working spaces and brand them as 'learning squares', analogous to the corporate 'office landscape'.[11] Here, perhaps a well-meant desire to create less hierarchical situations, which originally informed these architectural interventions, too easily blended with the current obsession with connecting spaces, people and things in oversimplified projections of the networked nature of individual and social life. No doubt, once a connection has been established, it must be reaffirmed over and over again, to the point at which distraction becomes the paradigmatic mode of attention. However, even in distraction there is an opportunity to study, I realised while hanging out in the Willem

---

10 Political philosopher Hannah Arendt conceptualised the so-called 'active life' of humans (as opposed to the thinking or contemplative life) through the notions of labour, work and action in *The Human Condition*, first published in 1958. While labour sustains life and work builds and maintains a world for human use, only action allows humans to actualise freedom.

11 'Office landscapes' were originally introduced in Germany in the 1950s as large, open-plan office spaces and remain a common occurrence in corporate architecture, despite

de Kooning Academy's office landscape, chatting with two colleagues. We discussed the Netflix show *Chef's Table*, a series of documentaries about the heads of kitchens of well-known restaurants. We watched the trailer of an episode portraying pastry chef Jordi Roca.[12] Whispering with a voice that never fully recovered after a serious case of laryngitis, he notes, 'When you are silent, you learn a lot.' Harney and Moten teach us that to study means to chime in with the dynamic always-going-on of a social space. For Jordi Roca learning is what you do privately, in silence, defining your own criteria with regards to the change you allow, seek or enforce. We should practise silence much more at our schools.

***

No doubt the value of art projects such as Art School lies in the opportunity they create for students to engage with contemporary art—not as something to learn about, but as an occasion to study. Just by looking at the documentation it becomes evident that art can be a way to invite students to develop a more reflective attitude towards their school and the place where they live. They do so by exercising a much wider range of actions than education typically encourages. I see the students drawing, cutting, building, discussing, trying, failing, walking, obstructing, lifting, collaborating, jumping, squatting, measuring, lying down, waiting, chatting, listening, writing, observing, modelling, playing, testing, styling, eating, thinking, running, scratching, scribbling, pushing, applauding, bending, taping, circling, combing, researching, showing, organising, provoking, smiling—and I could go on for a while. How can we, in a similar way, also become students, I wonder? With this question in mind, Rhona and I set up a brief exchange of work and ideas to activate some of the questions the aforementioned projects deal with, but in my context this time. A double cap from the Huddlewear series,

controversies around their effect on health and productivity of employees. 'Learning squares' represent a move away from traditional classrooms, first introduced during the large-scale reforms in secondary education in the Netherlands of the late 1990s, intended to stimulate self-directed learning of students—the so-called 'New Learning'. A 'learning square' is an open-plan space, designed for a large group of students, working on tasks, individually or in groups, supervised by one or several teachers.

which puts the two people who wear it in close proximity to each other, travelled to a new environment, my academy, where I could activate it with a group of students. However, the double cap, as an outcome of a larger project, does not necessarily fully disclose the questions that informed the process leading up to the production of the work. Nor does it demonstrate working strategies used in the classroom, while working with the students. Therefore, every day, for the period of a week, I received a proposition, which I could perform myself and forward to my students. This created a space for a real engagement with, and a conversation about, the strategies of the artist. It also allowed for more distracted responses into completely different directions. A space for study, so to say, revolving around rehearsal and practice, rather than representation. Similarly, rather than reporting on things that happened elsewhere, I'd like this text to be such a space too. Below, dear reader, you can find the seven propositions that made up the displaced rehearsal of the process of exploring the tension between personal and social space, between thought and behaviour—and many other notions that you may or may not have encountered above already. Among other places, the propositions have been practised in Blessington, Ireland, and Rotterdam, the Netherlands. You are kindly invited to use them as well, as an occasion to study. And, as you will see, they end with silence.

***

Monday. Proposition 1:
'Try to stand that little bit closer to things and people than you normally would.'

Tuesday. Proposition 2:
'Count how many thresholds you pass through today.'

Whether these educational reforms and architectural interventions produced anything better than previous forms of education did remains a controversial issue.

12 'Jordi Roca' is episode 3, season 4 of *Chef's Table*, and was first aired 13 April 2018.

Wednesday. Proposition 3:
'Find formal and informal gatherings of people. See how you can join them. Make a gathering.'

Thursday. Proposition 4:
'Experiment with the volume of your voice.'

Friday. Proposition 5:
'Draw a circle on the ground that marks your comfort zone. Measure it.'

Saturday. Proposition 6:
'Make a safe place for one person. Make a safe place for one insect.'

Sunday. Proposition 7:
'Gather a group of people and go for a long (1hr+) silent walk. On return, make a long collective drawing in silence, mapping the experience and journey.'

Art, the body and time perspective(s) in the classroom
Annemarie Ní Churreáin

CURRICULUM

Behind the gates, a black awakening of trees.

Were you made to kneel here too, Mary, Josephine, Bernadette?
If I call you by your house-names will you speak?[1]

Curriculum, a word with Latin roots, means first of all *to race* or *during the course of a race*, and derives from the verb *currere*, meaning *to run/ to proceed*. As a poet who is sometimes invited to visit primary and secondary schools, I try to convey to students that competition, success, the clock's hand are not contrary to the language and landscape of Art. Yes my poems are primarily rooted in memory, orientated by what Milan Kundera described as 'the secret bond between slowness and remembering'.[2] But in actuality the ethic powering my practice is largely future-focused. Out of this push and pull comes metaphor, musicality, meaning. Art happens *anyway*, despite and often because of constraint(s), and mostly my life as a writer is premised on daily experiences of time that wider society misconstrues as the enemy of Art. Practice is born more often out of labour than it is of freedom. 'Do not be an artist because you want to be free… You are already free. When you start to be an artist you enter a discipline.'[3]

In an assessment of how the digital revolution has altered time perspectives, renowned psychologist Professor Philip Zimbardo argues that there now exists a growing conflict in mainstream schools between increasingly present-orientated minds with a need to control and navigate space, and an outmoded, largely future-orientated system that promotes passivity and delay of gratification.[4] Certainly in my own school workshops the present moment is hotly contested. It is the teacher's job to propel the student forward across the present moment line as quickly as possible;

---

1   Annemarie Ní Churreáin, 'Bloodroot', *Bloodroot* (Inverin: Doire Press, 2017).
2   Milan Kundera, *Slowness*, trans. Linda Asher (New York: Harpercollins Publishers, 1996).
3   Leigh Hobba, 'Out of the Analogue', *Australian Perspecta*, exhibition, AGNSW, 1996.
4   Philip Zimbardo, 'RSA Animate: The Secret Powers of Time', RSA Lectures, 2010.

it is often the student's desire to secure sole influence over the present moment. Within this scenario the artist's task is to assist students to reorder time—to stop, slow, still, speed and connect with a perspective authentic to one's own understanding of time (and to do so within a future-focused environment determined by inflexible parameters).

But despite these tricksy dynamics, the school classroom does seem to me to be a place better than many others for writing poetry or engaging students in creative work. Making art is, after all, a somewhat unwieldy process by which, against the odds, more than two things are always happening at once. In a poem words invoke past, but also move the poem's body forward. Lines are broken to separate, but also to conjoin. Breath connects and separates. Art is both a making of and a giving in to mystery. We invent and we concede, at once losing and finding, with the hope that out of this *strain* an unexpected thing will reveal itself. Conflict seems not only unavoidable but perhaps essential to the whole endeavour and craft. One might say that at the heart of Art School, the student body is engaged in a type of reconfiguration or disruption of time perspective(s).

'Every word,' Böll said, 'has a great burden of memories, not only just of one person but of all mankind.'[5] In opening up a conversation with my students I ordinarily begin by asking them to consider the currency of individual words, the idea that every word, no matter how ordinary or everyday, is haunted by histories that are unknowable to us. Even words lightly spoken, like *desk*, *door*, *chalk*, carry an electricity that at times may be witnessed by the poet, or felt, but never fully understood. It is always a rich challenge to draw students' attention towards this past-life 'burden', while at the same time encouraging them to look forward into the future that the poem aspires to (a future that should maintain some distance from the poet's own conscious desires). In thinking about creative practice, the body and time perspectives in the classroom, I am compelled to ask certain questions: what does it mean to cultivate creative

---

5   A. Leslie Willson, interview with Heinrich Böll, 'The Art of Fiction No. 1974', *The Paris Review* 87 (Spring 1983).

thinking and autonomy within a highly controlled environment? How is school-time experienced inside the workshop? Is it part of my job as arts facilitator to help students unlearn, if even for a moment, future-focused time perspectives? If so, why?

> *Torn avenue and pillars either side,   I am here for the girl*
> *who had birds in her eyes.*
> *If I render a wing may she speak?*

On the subject of images and metaphor, I recently quoted Irish-born poet Lola Ridge to a class of teenagers, by scrawling the following words large on the whiteboard: 'Write anything that burns.' Students were asked to comment on how this advice might or might not be useful for beginner writers. Interpreting the words literally at first, the class dismissed the idea as useless, irresponsible even, i.e. 'write what harms you' and 'write what causes you to feel pain'. But slowly, as we excavated and contextualised the burden of the words, students arrived at the deeper conclusion that fire observes a world of ancient and tribal tradition, generates power, may evoke a sense of origin, godliness, source.

Other? Other* Other!, an Art School project in which the artist Vanessa Donoso López developed a series of workshops at Gaelscoil de hÍde and Scoil Mhuire, also unfurled connections to past landscapes and times. Introducing the architecture of Antoni Gaudí, López asked students to consider what it means to be a stranger in another country, suggesting that 'one way of dealing with homesickness is to become familiar with your surroundings'. Students learned how and in what ways mountain clay is more 'fun' than machine-made clay, and created hexagon-shaped ceramic tiles imprinted with local flowers, plants and other objects. This marking of landscape as a means of relating home to loss was for me resonant of the scarring of language into physical earth by Ogham—an

Early Medieval tree-based script used to write the Irish language (and in some rare instances found in Spain).[6] All surviving Ogham inscriptions in Ireland are inscribed on stone.

'Nothing is art if it does not come from nature,' Gaudí said, and, 'originality consists in returning to the origin. The straight line belongs to men, the curved one to God.'[7] On many occasions I have felt daunted by the lack of historical memory that school students bring to the endeavour of writing poems. Yet through López's project I am reminded that memory is not linear and is defined differently by different spaces. Past is carried too in bone and earth. Memory may be tactile. In *Other? Other* Other!* students brought the physical self to this exploration of hindsight perspective, literally imprinting the body on the past. In an environment where touching, hugging, running and other physical expression may be censored, this sensual and autonomous bodily experience appears particularly potent. At the same time, individual tiles slotted together like puzzle pieces, drawing attention to the practical nature of fitting in, of belonging to a specific place in time and of mediating between self, wildness and a wider system. López described fired tiles as 'glass-like', suggesting that one may look backwards or forwards *into* time through the newly made object. For this project, López chose not to fire the tiles; they were left instead to disintegrate. In another workshop López's students inserted similar tiles into the landscape, treading upon them and, over time, witnessing decay and disappearance. Perhaps not unlike the unfired clay tile, a piece of free or unedited writing produced in a workshop illustrates perfectly the strange labour of remembering and unremembering ourselves into the past.

Father with two red seeds in your palms,
if I show you my bones spilling out
will you show me a stone in this yard that can speak?

6 Crístoír M. Fhearaigh, *Ogham: An Irish Alphabet* (New York: Hippocrene Books, 1998).
7 Juan Bassegoda Nonell, *Antonio Gaudí: Master Architect* (New York: Abbeville Press, 2000).

What is the relationship between landscape and lyrical control? Between control and imagination? Between the place that I physically come from and the state in which I, as a woman in Ireland today, now exist? In my practice these questions have allowed me to interrogate the experience of growing up on rural bogland with a language shaped over time by decay, loss and burial.

In *Still life snap shot*,[8] another Art School workshop series led by artist Jane Fogarty, students were introduced to artworks as a form of clock, with time as a concept measured and visualised in alternative ways. Using images of petrified trees and other natural objects alongside images with a much less condensed history, students were guided through a series of exercises, timing themselves as they manipulated clay, poured paint, created physical manifestations of the present moment. In this reimaging of time as object, time was rendered public and external. 'I wanted students to be able to physically hold something and regard it for its temporal qualities in addition to / beyond its aesthetic values.'[9]

Class timetables, intercom announcements, exam dates: term time locks the body out of natural, wild or intuitive flows of time and into a mode that I consider artificial and punctuated by an abrupt, stop-start rhythm. Looming always is lunchtime, class-end time, the time at which pens, thoughts, conversations drop instantly in shutdown of one moment before the beginning of another. This atmosphere in which every single second counts chimes easily with digital culture anxieties around speed; the speed of downloads, of connection, of reply. What resonated most with me about Fogarty's workshop was the scope within the engagement to experience the process of waiting, to reconcile oneself to what otherwise might translate as time *wasted*.

Wasted time or time unaccounted for in productivity terms is of particular value to me as a poet, the time to be bored, to obsess and ideally to become for a while lost. Loss as a theme is central, and is at

---

8 Jane Fogarty, *Still life snap shot*, Roscommon, 2016.
9 Jane Fogarty, from personal email correspondences with Annemarie Ní Churreáin (27 May 2019).

work always in the way I count syllables, break text, separate verses. In my poems I strip, part and pare to free new meaning and move the reader backward and forward through real and imagined time. In my school workshops, students are encouraged to use white space on the page to experiment with loss or fragmentation of memory. Similarly, in reading poems aloud, breath becomes an instrument and device of silence, allowing the performer to regulate how time is passed and how long it takes, for example, for an idea to take shape in the world.

Still life snap shot opened up a space inside the classroom with the potential for students to experience stillness, to (re)orientate within the present moment, to quite literally grasp time in the form of a physical object. It considered education as a cumulative process comprising individual moments of time and the self, inside those individual moments, as narrator. 'Autobiography begins with a sense of being alone,' Berger said.[10] 'It is an orphan form.' This is an idea underpinning many of my own classroom workshops, that of the orphan self as the maker of foundations, with autobiography providing an inroad into a wide variety of worlds, including fiction, mythologies and research.

> *Doors if I stitch you a collar of lace all Spring*
> *as I wait for the first-born*
> *heat   please,   won't you open and speak?*

What is school for? What was school for? What will school be for? For *The Masterplan,* an Art School partnership with Educate Together National School Dublin 7, artists Ella De Búrca and John Beattie worked with students who are (at the time of writing) temporarily located in Grangegorman Lower and awaiting relocation to a new school site. Using the theme of *transition*, the artists developed a spoken-word opera with students, drawing heavily upon improvisation and gesture for the

---

[10] John Berger, 'Her Secrets', in *Hiding in Plain Sight: Essays in Criticism and Autobiography*, ed. Wendy Lesser (San Francisco: Mercury House, 1993).

final performance. In musical terms the concept of transition refers to the passing of one key to another, but also to a passage that takes the composition from one key into another… a transient modulation; a passage leading from one motif to the next.

To the written word the human body brings the keys of silence, breath and sound. *The Masterplan* harmonised a chorus of bodies, allowing bodies to slip in and out of time with each other. In my own poetry recitals the body is often used to reclaim historical loss by becoming, in a public space, the navigator of pause, wordlessness, silence. Most notably within prison workshops (and with other students in the care of the state), silence is a device for excavation and for facing the experience of lifelessness. An openness to death and/or dying is central to the spirit of poems read aloud. The held breath conserves the spirit; the exhaled breath gifts it. Perhaps this concept, based loosely on the principles of yin and yang, is best described by poet Li-Young Lee, who says,

> a poem is a musical score for the voice. The voice is ultimately the reticulated dying breath. Therefore, every poem is a score for the dying breath. If you examine the nature of speech, you will notice that when I breathe in I'm full of life and as I breathe out I may begin to talk. The more I talk, the less breath I have but the more meaning gets made. Meaning increases in opposite ratio to vitality.[11]

---

[11] Li-Young Lee, from 'The 2014 Caesar and Patricia Tabet Poetry Reading Series' at the Creative Media Lab, Dominican University.

Using a group exercise, spoken-word opera students also engaged in a game of word-relay, exploring how words become gnarled and reshaped, and how information, over time, passed from body to body, is lost and reimagined. Reflecting upon this exercise, I am called to think about the way in which songs and poems have traditionally in Ireland been gifted, on the dying breath, down through the generations. Implicit in these 'by heart' gifts is the fact of the body and a type of faith that is poetically sensitive to the concept of an afterlife.

Following *The Masterplan* workshops and performances, an exhibition titled *It's Very New School* took place at Rua Red Gallery. For this iteration of the project, the artists created a floating shelf displaying a series of custom-made books, each book spine imprinted with students' responses and questions around the purpose of school. Among the titles were: *A Place for Disciplining Children*; *For Learning How to Learn*; *For Making Sure the Future Generations Will Be Equipped with the Right Tools to Improve the World*. This reclamation of the books and text, and the chance to become creator of knowledge rather than simply consumer of knowledge, echoes the 'by heart' dying breath and the possibility of a life after this present moment.

Home, if I press my lips to your ruins *three times*
and circle the grounds like a beast, *if I say my root*
to this earth

who will hear when I speak?

'How long does it take to write a poem? How many poems are in a book? What percentage of the retail price does a poet take from the sale of each book?' In the classroom these are typically the first questions asked of me about poetry. Even the youngest student, in a language that is often inarticulate yet still curiously perceptive, is grappling with the math of what I do in an attempt to measure what finally the artist has to show for this mysterious labour in units of time. But the artwork alone best accounts for its own making, and only the poem can demonstrate the true value of the poet's time. When I read aloud, attention is turned in towards the body, the mouth, the expelled breath. The poem arising from or within the classroom places the body back at the centre of the student experience, placing the student experience back at the centre of the curriculum. For the New School artist, and in my own practice as a poet in the classroom, art brings to the *race* of learning new momentum, a reconfigured understanding of discipline, the potential for an altered perspective of the course.

Preparatory gestures for a future curriculum
Clare Butcher

Prologue

The following text could be read as an analysis of the process around Sarah Pierce's collaborative project *The Square* (2015), gleaned from unpublished video documentation, a few participant responses and in conversation with the artist. While attending to particular materials, methods and bodies at work, the analysis is unfaithful, veering off into reflection and back to description with some misleading cues. Rather than focusing on *what* happens in the process, there is a special interest in *how* it happens and where the frameworks of conceptualisation and instruction become blurred with the performance of everyday personal positions and possible action on a school gymnasium-turned-stage.

Preparation

> Gymnasium
> Black paint
> Rollers, coveralls (never enough for every individual in group—always negotiated)
> Stir-stick
> Time (it takes as long as it takes)
> Camera on tripod

Introduction
In rows. Behaved bodies sit on benches. The stranger stands, facing them. Hands gesturing in circles, over and over, as she describes the way she works. Pointing out the benches. The rows. The postures. The structures at play. The bodies turn to look at the camera. The stranger shakes each of their hands.

And so begins the first of six Tuesday sessions in Sarah Pierce's artist residency at Blessington Community College. The project has multiple frames. One being that it forms Sarah's contribution to the ongoing series Art School initiated by Jennie Guy (Jennie's the one behind the camera). Another frame is that these mornings with a group of Transition Year students take place within the more regular school curriculum,[1] with its disciplinary ideologies and modes of self-regulating, as well as the expectation that engagements with art make students learn 'self-expression'. Each session is recorded on video from different positions within the school gymnasium. The only other witness to this process of producing a play with no audience.

Drawing on the model of the *'Lehrstück'* developed by Bertolt Brecht in the first decades of the last century, the 'learning play'—or as it's sometimes translated, the 'teaching play'—is one in which actors become students of repeated gesture, of the possibilities of improvisation, and spectators of their own process. With the intention of 'showing how things work',[2] this methodology attempts to make visible the structures in which art and work appear, arguably inspired by the materialist cynicism of Brecht's contemporaneous Russian ex-Futurists. By highlighting the power of interactive forces such as those between labourer-actor and the script, infrastructure and event, the apparatus of production could be exposed. Confronting entertainment value with a kind of performative pedagogy, Brecht required that participants/spectators in his *Lehrstücke* acquire attitudes rather than aim for a finished, presentable piece,[3] in an endless rehearsing of possible responses and relationships. It's said that Brecht would circulate questionnaires following each learning play, and would rewrite the script based on the feedback received.

Instructions
Instructions are given with stir-stick as prop. A baton to

---

1 Transition Year is an optional one-year programme after students in Ireland complete their Junior Certificate. Interestingly, the mission statement of the Transition Year reads as: 'To promote the personal, social, educational and vocational development of pupils and to prepare them for their role as autonomous, participative and responsible members of society.' For more details see: *Rules and Programme for Secondary Schools*, Department of Education and Science, Ireland, 2004.
2 Stanley Mitchell, 'Introduction', in *Understanding Brecht*, trans. Anna Bostock (London:

coordinate future gestures. To be painted: a 2x2 metre square. No tools of measurement but the body and the space around it.

The form taken by this first exercise gives the project its name, and becomes a catalyst for future actions. Collectively negotiated by the student/actors, some wearing overalls, some not, they teeter on each other's shoulders and find wobbly benches to paint the full height of the shape. Perhaps this interaction is of more consequence than the art historical reference made in repeating the iconic shape. Less consequential but still significant. Malevich's staging of the *Black Square* (1915) was made infamous by a documentation image of the painting presiding over what was deemed to be *The Last Futurist Exhibition*.[4] I've never seen any of the four originals. And it's not about that.

This, *The Square*, will remain on the wall throughout the sessions with Sarah Pierce and act as a backdrop to other events in the gymnasium: morning assembly, PE classes, after-school activities, the black box performative space of the everyday. As the only evidential 'outcome' of the process, some school staff members reach for the metrics of its possible assessment. An example of 'being literate'? 'Being creative'? 'Working with others'? Skills to be acquired by each student for their Leaving Certificate.[5] Challenging these assessment criteria, *The Square* insists on its own opacity in terms of what it might *mean*, and offers functionality instead, in terms of what it might *do*.

Interruption
A different group enters the space. All heads turn to look.
Outside the camera's field of vision.

In another gymnasium, over the water and within a different kind of

Verso, 1998), xv.
3 Ibid.
4 *The Last Futurist Exhibition of Paintings 0,10* was installed in Petrograd in late 1915. The infamous exhibition-view documentation featured Malevich's *Black Square* hung in what would usually be the 'holy corner' in Christian Orthodox homes. More context around this exhibition and Malevich's 'Suprematism' can be found in Jane Sharp's essay. PDF available at monoskop.org, Jane Sharp, 'The Critical Reception of the 0.10

institutional mise en scène—a school within a school (more on this in a moment)—a group of volunteer student-actor-hopefuls gather for an audition that's not an audition. By pitching up, you've got a part. A mixture of faith and curiosity has brought many there to play the roles of townsfolk in the making of a new city.[6] The project is part of the School of Missing Studies, a temporary programme hosted within the Sandberg Institute, which is an ongoing curriculum built around responsive approaches to '[calls] for a space to turn existing knowledge against itself to affect our capacity to see things otherwise, to trust that seeing, and to set one's own pedagogical terms'.[7] Initiated by artist duo Bik Van der Pol, the space of the school holds enquiries into not only what the structure of an MFA educational process around 'the missing' might be, but also into the deceptively less visible structures that bring us together as citizens, as institutionalised beings, as life-long learners. Sarah Pierce is here too. In the wings, so to speak.[8]

Based on similarly didactic principles to the *Lehrstücke*,[9] these actor-hopefuls are working on the script of Brecht's operetta *The Rise and Fall of the City of Mahagonny*: a story of grand human undertakings and the power of nature (human and non-human) to undo them. Originally staged by its scenographer, Casper Neher, on a boxing ring—another kind of black square—the space of civic negotiation is transposed in this case into the subterranean gym-turned-rehearsal studio/dancefloor, where the student group riff irreverently on the operetta's libretto in front of the camera. 'Every great endeavour has its ups and downs, every great endeavour has its ups and downs...' And we're reminded that 'quoting a text implies interrupting its context', as Walter Benjamin writes in his analysis of Brecht's 'epic theatre'.[10] Their lifted citations are interrupted by editing later, spliced together with footage of construction sites and blueprints, making words and gestures strange to one another in yet one more recontextualisation.[11]

Exhibition: Malevich and Benua', 1992 (accessed 12 May 2020).
5   See Turlough O'Donnell's remarks in Jennie Guy, with Thomas Fitzpatrick, Gary Granville, Turlough O'Donnell and Sarah Pierce, 'Art School: An Exchange', in Niamh Dunphy, Nathan O'Donnell, Adrian Duncan and Marysia Wieckiewicz-Carroll ed., *Paper Visual Art Journal* 8 (2017): 31–2.
6   This audition was part of a film, *Men Are Easier to Manage Than Rivers* (2015), made during my MFA with the School of Missing Studies as a collaboration with BA students

Citation
The figure points to different bodies in the room.
'Say something to the square.' 'What's already been said?'
'Listen to what's been said.'
'You're a flag.'
'You're patchy.'
'You're a rainbow.'
'You're not square.'

Back in Blessington, as students in the group are invited to respond to the form they've painted on the wall. Some boldly, some quietly, they attend to the physical appearance of the form and its imperfections, linking the contrast of colour and minimal shape to complex experiences of body shaming, gender identity, bullying, fear of the other, rejection. Through active listening, the statements get recirculated, repeated, reproduced by other voices in the group. Good body memory skill-development perhaps, but more importantly here is that the responses-turned-citations are transformed into a chorus of shared experience: the beginnings of a collective script.

After reflecting on what was spoken, what was heard, what was done, the stranger invites the larger group to divide into smaller cells and exercise some collective responses. Scattered through the gymnasium. Posing in group formations. Some spin. Some stretch out their arms to touch the other. In these compositions, the citations are workshopped by the groups into scenes. Small tableaux vivants emerge as the student / actors articulate the terms and movements of the process thus far. This articulation is not only a matter of utterance but also a more functional approach in which those terms and movements are divided into joints for further exercise.

whom I was teaching at the time.
7 See Bik Van der Pol, ed., *School of Missing Studies* (Berlin: Sternberg Press, 2017). The School of Missing Studies MFA programme ran from 2013 to 2015 in Amsterdam. More information can be found at sandberg.nl, Temporary Programmes, The School of Missing Studies.
8 Under the supervision of Sarah Pierce and Ellen C. Feiss, the project culminated in a short musical film and thesis, *Prompt Book*.

Epic articulation
'Just try to figure out what's next.'
Mise en scène is limited to ten gestures. Voices mumble, some giggle nervously. In a circle, their backs to the middle. Facing out. A figure paces the circumference, listening intently, deciphering words from hubbub.
The voices of the group rise with each other.

In an article subtitled 'Stalking the Politics of the Hidden Curriculum', Henry Giroux identifies a common thread running through various pedagogical enquiries around 'those unstated norms, values, and beliefs embedded in and transmitted to students through the underlying rules that structure the routines and social relationships in school and classroom life'.[12] While the awareness of these conditions is imperative, Giroux argues that to be useful, the concept of the hidden curriculum needs retooling, and should 'link approaches to human consciousness and action to forms of structural analysis that explore how [reproduction and transformation] interpenetrate each other rather than appear as separate pedagogical concerns'.[13] The *Lehrstück* enters the classroom. Less spotlit, and with more care, the lessons of the teaching play become a mutual unlearning of power structures. Out of the black box and within the walls of everyday institutionalised experience, the claiming of agency becomes more than a performative gesture.

In her project which takes up *The Hidden Curriculum*, artist Annette Krauss investigates the 'unidentified, unintended and unrecognized forms of knowledge, values and beliefs in the context of secondary school education', particularly 'the physicality of education… [and] everything that is learned alongside the official curriculum'.[14] Her project pays particular attention to the coping strategies students

---

9   See Erika Hugh, 'Brecht's Lehrstücke and Drama Education', in *Key Concepts in Theater/Drama Education* (New York: Springer, 2011), 197.
10 Walter Benjamin, *Understanding Brecht*, trans. Anna Bostock (London: Verso, 1998), 19.
11 *Men Are Easier to Manage Than Rivers* (2015) was my MFA project produced in the context of the School of Missing Studies, under the supervision of Sarah Pierce… where this conversation began. For more on the project see academia.edu, Clare Butcher, 'Men are Easier to Manage than Rivers—A Prompt Book'.

develop to subordinate hierarchy and counter the silent violences of every day. Racism, abortion, low income, depression—are just some of those violences named by the students around *The Square*.

> *Rehearsal*
> *Act One*
> *'Square, because of your colour I was scared,' says one student. 'You are a unique shape of square,' observes another. 'Who did this to you?'*

'I'm not asking you to become social workers in this moment,' says the stranger who is now not so strange. 'It's about giving yourselves time to ask that question.' The power of asking 'who did this to you?'—as one of many questions emerging from institutionalised experience—together with the minimal score of pared-down gestures, expose and propose the mechanisms of rehearsing and preserving the self-in-school. Having gone through a process of identifying, articulating and then sharing these mechanisms, the tableaux of each act around *The Square* could be read as a protocol for maintaining personal dignity and some kind of solidarity within structures of social control and the reproduction of values. Another kind of curriculum perhaps, though placing a name like that on this assembly of intimate proportions seems inappropriate.

But these protocols are not one-size-fits-all. They are situated, interactive. Particular to the idiosyncrasies of the structures surrounding the bodies who constitute them. This was one iteration of the project, and when Sarah Pierce interpreted *The Square* in other contexts—in an exhibition setting, in a summer school for young curators[15]—the mechanisms had to change. The young curators found some of the methods in the process to be 'schoolish', and needed to work through their own emotional experiences of what it is to learn how to do something

---

12 Henry Giroux, 'Schooling and the Myth of Objectivity: Stalking the Politics of the Hidden Curriculum', *McGill Journal of Education / Revue des sciences de l'éducation de McGill* [s.l.] 16, no. 3 (September 1981): 286.
13 Giroux, 'Schooling and the Myth of Objectivity', 296.
14 Interview by Hannah Jickling and Helen Reed with Annette Krauss. Available at thepedagogicalimpulse.com, The Living Archive, 'Documenting Secrets'.
15 Exhibition curated by Jennie Guy at Rua Red, *It's Very New School*, 2017; and 5th

together. And the Tallaght Community Arts youth group, who usually practise in a theatre context, had to contend with working in an exhibition space for the first time—with all its historical baggage and less obvious forms of performativity. Interestingly, the neighbourhood around that exhibition hosts another 'The Square'—a shopping mall and a stage for both coming together as young people but also the last tram stop from the city centre, reminding the area's mainly newcomer inhabitants of their place on the edge of things.[16]

These negotiations and situations are not readily available in documentation, traceable in an artist or academic archive. There is something to be said for *Lehrstück* logic here. As the project reiterates itself, moving through different gestures, different words, different structures, the protocols multiply in different bodies. Those exercises in recognising power and embodying a response to it could become muscle memories in ways that go beyond measurable skills development. One cell, one ligament, one shift in perception at a time. Beyond individual coping mechanisms, the force of such a co-authored curriculum of embodied self-care, rather than a generalised notion of 'empowerment', could operate in the understanding that particular conditions are usually symptomatic of a larger complex experienced by many. Ways to meet those conditions for oneself, and together, could be found in these preparatory gestures for a situated social justice.

Collapse
And rise. Collapse and rise. The bodies move through the final acts of their learning play. Huddling, hovering. They link arms and fill the latitude of the space. Finally forming a single row, side by side, down on the floor. They whisper to no one and one another. Their breath hangs in the air.
'We have no shame.'

Curatorial Moscow Summer School, 2016.
16 The Square Tallaght shopping mall complex was opened in 1990, and is set to expand in the coming years to 200,000ft^2 of retail space.

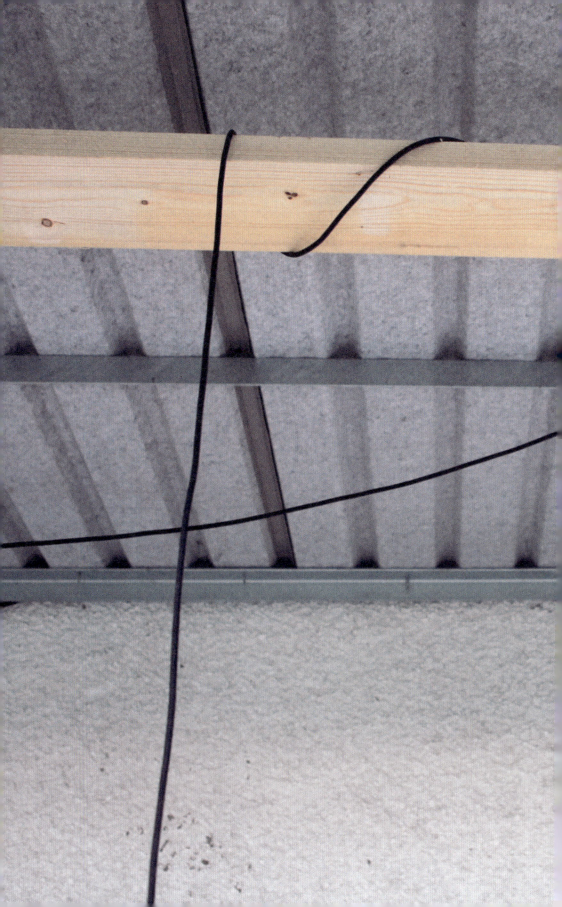

Acknowledgements

This is a space to acknowledge everyone who has contributed to this book, as well as everyone who has been a part of the evolution of Art School over the years. I feel overwhelmed as I bring this list of collaborators and contributors to the page for the first time, as both *Curriculum* and Art School have been formed by a host of talented people, who have played both visible and invisible roles and supported these projects in a variety of ways. I see this book as a celebration of each and all of these, and of the ecology that has unfolded between.

To begin, I would like to thank all of the students, artists, host schools, educators, assistants, audiences, respondents, partners and funders who have collaboratively shaped, shared and made possible the Art School projects that are the seeds from which this book has grown. There are more specific thanks within specific projects included further into this section, but I wanted to start by extending this special thanks, in particular, to all of the students who have contributed their imagination, passion, energy and sense of experimentation to these projects. Their ongoing role in these projects—and in this book—can not be emphasised enough.

This book is a space in which a multitude of voices converge, and in which both a collective celebration and critique of art and education have been able to take form. I want to thank the writers who have contributed to this book, for trusting in the ambitions of the project and tracing the writers' brief outwards through so many different subjects and territories. Thanks to Clare Butcher, Juan Canela, Helen Carey, Daniela Cascella, Andrew Hunt, Hannah Jickling and Helen Reed, Alissa Kleist, Rowan Lear, Peter Maybury, Annemarie Ní Churreáin, Nathan O'Donnell, Sofía Olascoaga and Priscila Fernandes, Matt Packer and Sjoerd Westbroek, who have been such a pleasure to work with, and who have each given such consideration to the spirit of the project. I also want to thank Gerard Byrne for his considered conversations along the way, and for providing such an insightful opening to the book through his foreword.

Developing this book has been both a rewarding and a challenging journey, and I am indebted to the core team of collaborators who have invested their talent and energy in its production. I am eternally thankful to my assistant book editor Fiona Gannon for being such an attentive reader and collaborator, for her calming presence, her assurance, her endurance and her incredible imagination and intuition as a writer and editor. I want to thank my copy-editor Neil Burkey for his precision, his attention to detail and his open-door policy with so many wayward textual fragments. I owe my thanks to Sage Anderson for her wise suggestions and incisive edits, and for making me laugh by asking: *Why do people make books?* Thanks to Peter Maybury for all of his work and dedication designing this book, and for helping to coax such a complicated set of ideas into such a beautiful form. I am thankful to both Sarah Pierce and David Crowley for kindly sharing their experience and providing guidance along the way, as their advice has shaped this book and enabled it to evolve to its full potential to reach as wide a readership as it deserves. With this in mind, I want to thank everyone at Intellect Books for the opportunity to work with them on the distribution of *Curriculum*, and to extend a special thanks to Mareike Wehner and Tim Mitchell for being so supportive and encouraging throughout the process of preparing this book for publication. I also want to express my gratitude to my partner Sven Anderson for his continued insight and presence throughout this process, and for always being there with me as the book moved backwards and forwards (and backwards, and forwards), and finally towards completion.

I want to thank each and every artist (and curator) who has so generously opened their practice to younger collaborators and audiences through Art School over the years. I don't think that the role of art within any social context can be overplayed, and there is so much to celebrate having worked together in different schools over the past five years. Thanks to Sven Anderson, John Beattie, Clare Breen, Sarah Browne, Karl Burke, Rhona Byrne, Ella de Búrca, Vanessa Donoso López, Priscila Fernandes, Hannah Fitz, Jane Fogarty, Kevin Gaffney, Fiona Hallinan, Elaine Leader, Maria McKinney, Maeve Mulrennan, Mark O'Kelly, Sarah Pierce, Naomi Sex and Orlaith Treacy.

There are a host of people and projects that are not explicitly mentioned in the essays that comprise this book but that have nonetheless been crucially involved in the thinking and motivation that has supported this project since its inception. The following list gathers those seemingly endless supportive forces who have given and continue to give momentum to the collective life of the project, and whose gestures still stir its futural becoming.

Firstly, I am grateful to the Arts Council of Ireland and the arts office of Wicklow County Council for funding the production of this book. Without their generous support, none of this would be possible. I want to thank Wicklow County arts officer Jenny Sherwin for her continued engagement and support in relation to both the evolution of Art School and the development of *Curriculum*. I want to express my sincere gratitude to Ger Ó Sé for being a strong component of the project's initiation, as the first principal that I worked with (and continue to work with), and for trusting in my ability to bring this work to a new level through the Per Cent for Art commission in St Catherine's National School. I also want to thank Fingal County public arts manager Caroline Cowley for her support in the evolution of that commission. My thanks to project liaison and co-producer Linda Shevlin, for first bringing Art School nationwide to Roscommon, and for her co-production on events and documentation.

I would like to share my appreciation for teacher Turlough O'Donnell, for his enthusiasm and patience, and for helping me shape certain ideas each of the times that we worked together in Blessington Community College. I want to share my gratitude to Clodagh Kenny, for her generous invitation and trust in me to expand my research into wider fields of practice. I also would like to thank Helen O'Donoghue for sharing her expertise over the years. I am fortunate to have had the opportunity to work with Stine Marie Jacobsen on *Artists' Exercises*, an online platform for sharing fragments of artists' educational strategies with contributions from over fifty international artists ranging from Elizabeth Stephens and Annie Sprinkles' '25 Ways to Make Love to the Earth' to Stephen Brandes' '49 Ways to Change Your Home'. Lastly, my thanks to Cleo Fagan for her partnership through the Mobile Art School projects that took place between 2012 and 2014. It was through realising the strength of this work alongside the engagement and encouragement of various friends, colleagues and support systems (and even being included in President Michael D. Higgins' Ethics Initiative Seminar!) that the inception of Art School became such a clear next step.

Throughout its evolution, Art School has gathered energy through exchanges. Often these exchanges have been with practitioners who helped communicate the project to wider audiences, bringing visibility and new potential. With this in mind, I am grateful to the Arts in Education Portal for platforming Art School over the years and for profiling the project when the portal first launched in 2014. I would like to thank Visual Artists Ireland and Ann Bradley for their early work publicising the project through the Visual Artists' News Sheet. I want to thank and remember both Orla Kenny and Jason Oakley for their early support through these organisations in communicating about 1Art School—I feel so privileged to have had the good fortune to have worked with and been supported by both of these generous and wise spirits. I would like to thank Joanne Laws, Dr Brian Fay and Dr Gary Granville for their textual contributions to Art School publications over the years; also to Thomas Fitzpatrick, Dr Gary Granville, Nathan O'Donnell, Turlough O'Donnell and Sarah Pierce for contributing to the text 'Art School: An Exchange' for *Paper Visual Art Journal* Volume 8. Thank you to Helen Carey, Ailbhe Murphy and Fiona Whelan for their invitation to submit a text on 'Art School (How People Come Up with Ideas)', for inclusion in the publication *TransActions #2 (Field and Academy: Knowledge and Counter Knowledge in Socially Engaged Art)*. To Liz Burns, for her invitation to develop a presentation about Art School at Wexford Arts Centre. I also want to extend my thanks to Laura Smith for her videography and video editing, Barry Lynch for his video editing and Louis Haugh for his project photography. Finally a sincere thanks to Rossi McCauley and Distinctive Repetition for his work designing four limited-edition posters (as well as many other graphic elements) that reflected the energy and vitality of the project so beautifully.

Art School developed through a series of overlapping projects including residencies, workshop programmes, exhibitions and other events. The group of people who contributed to these projects—often in different roles—was always in flux. These next paragraphs are my attempt to remember and thank everyone and to recall these projects in loose chronological sequence.

The first Art School project took place in 2014 at Blessington Community College in County Wicklow in collaboration with Wicklow County Arts Office's *Thinking Visual* programme. Thanks to artists Sven Anderson and John Beattie, the 2014 Transition Year students, principal Kieran Burke, art teacher Turlough O'Donnell, all of the staff at Blessington Community College, artist liaison Maria McKinney, Fire Station Artists' Studios, Niamh O'Donnell and the Mermaid Arts Centre, Distinctive Repetition for the design of the limited-edition poster that was gifted to each participating student, arts officer Jenny Sherwin, arts office assistant Donna Carroll, the Wicklow County Arts Office and the Arts Council.

In 2015, Art School continued to work with *Thinking Visual* at Blessington Community College. Thanks to artists Elaine Leader and Sarah Pierce, the 2015 Transition Year students, principal Kieran Burke, art teacher Turlough O'Donnell, all of the staff at Blessington Community College, Niamh O'Donnell and the Mermaid Arts Centre, arts officer Jenny Sherwin, the Wicklow County Arts Office and the Arts Council.

Art School continued in 2015 through *Magnetic Fields* at Scoil Chonglais in Baltinglass, County Wicklow. Thanks to artists Sven Anderson, John Beattie and Michael West, all of the collaborating students from Second to Fifth Years, teachers Thomas Ahern and Anne Deeney Walker, all of the staff at Scoil Chonglais, Niamh O'Donnell and the Mermaid Arts Centre, arts officer Jenny Sherwin, the Wicklow County Arts Office and the Arts Council.

In 2015, Art School initiated its first project outside of Wicklow with *Other? Other* Other!* at Gaelscoil de hÍde and Scoil Mhuire National Schools in County Roscommon. Thanks to artists Rhona Byrne and Vanessa Donoso López, the Fourth through Sixth Class collaborators, the school teachers and staff who supported the project, principals Orla Ní Chuinneagan and Úna Feeley, artist assistants Nollaig Molloy and Breda Coyne, Linda Shevlin, the Roscommon Arts Centre, the county Artists in Schools Scheme and Roscommon County Council.

In 2016, Art School returned to Blessington Community College, County Wicklow for its third project, *The Student Body*. Thanks to artists Rhona Byrne and Maria McKinney, Transition Year student collaborators, principal Kieran Burke, art teachers Turlough O'Donnell and Tanya Twyford-Troy, all of the staff who supported the project, Niamh O'Donnell and the Mermaid Arts Centre, arts officer Jenny Sherwin and everyone at the Wicklow County Arts Office and the Arts Council.

Later in 2016, the Art School project *Bead Game* took place at Bray School Project and St Mary's and St Gerard's National Schools in County Wicklow, with support from the Wicklow County Arts Office's Strategic Partnerships Initiative as well as from the Arts Council. Thanks to artist Fiona Hallinan; collaborators Katy Fitzpatrick and Aislinn O'Donnell, who contributed to the residency through workshops around art and philosophy; artist assistant Aoife Irwin Moore; the Fifth Class students in Bray School Project and Fourth Class students in St Mary's and St Gerard's National Schools in Enniskerry; principals Carol Lanigan and John Connor; teachers and school staff Ruth Feeley, Jamie Finnerty, Claire Ryan, Annette Gleeson, John Clarke, David Lynch, Olivia Murphy; all of the staff who supported the project in each of these schools; The First 47 for designing the limited-edition poster; arts officer Jenny Sherwin, advisor Mary McAuliffe, arts office assistant Donna Carroll and the Wicklow County Arts Office.

Also in 2016, Art School launched *The Masterplan* with the Dublin 7 Educate Together National School, which was commissioned within '*...the lives we live*' as part of the Grangegorman Public Art Programme. Thank you to artists John Beattie and Ella de Búrca; the Fourth, Fifth and Sixth Class collaborating students; principal Trish Clerkin; the teachers and staff at Dublin 7 Educate Together, including Niamh Ní Chlochartaigh, Fiona Hyland, Eoin Vaughan, Ruth Fitzgerald, Paul Bermingham, Mary Beadle, Amy Dunican, Catherine Lovely and John Lovely; photographer Louis Haugh; artist and educator Brian Fay for his written contribution; the Lighthouse Cinema for support with the screening event; and to public art coordinator Jenny Haughton and the Grangegorman Development Agency.

Art School developed a residency with Marino Institute of Further Education and St Joseph's National School in 2016. Thanks to artist Vanessa Donoso López, the Second Class students, the teachers and staff at St Joseph's National School, educator Michael Flannery and Marino Institute of Education.

In 2016, Art School initiated a series of workshops with Tisrara, Brideswell and Feevagh National Schools in County Roscommon. Thanks to artists Jane Fogarty, Hannah Fitz and Kevin Gaffney; the student artist collaborators; principals Aoife Donnelly, Carmel Kelly and Larry Tiernan; artist assistants Marion Balfe, Niamh O'Doherty and Anthony Keigher; the staff at each of the schools; curator-in-residence Linda Shevlin; and Roscommon County Council.

In 2017, Art School organised the residency *How to Swim on Dry Land* with Killinarden Community School in Tallaght, South County Dublin. Thank you to artist Sarah Browne, the Fifth Year student collaborators, principal Adrienne Whelan, art teacher Sarah Edmondson, the staff at Killinarden Community School, arts officer Orla Scannell and South Dublin County Council.

The Art School residency *Image of the Self With and Amongst Others* took place in Our Lady's School in Terenure, County Dublin in 2017. Thanks to artist Mark O'Kelly, Transition Year student collaborators, principal Pauline Meany, teachers Andrew Kenny and Dee Maguire, the staff at Our Lady's School, arts officer Orla Scannell and South Dublin County Council.

Running from 2016 into 2017, Art School initiated *I'll Be in Your Camp—Will You Be in Mine?* in collaboration with St Paul's CBS and Technological University Dublin (TUD) Grangegorman, which was commissioned within *'...the lives we live'* as part of the Grangegorman Public Art Programme. Thanks to artists Karl Burke and Naomi Sex, all of the student collaborators, principal Patrick McCormack, vice principal John Keane, art teacher Danielle Heffernan, the staff at TUD and St Paul's Christian Brothers School, and to public art coordinator Jenny Haughton and the Grangegorman Development Agency.

It's Very New School, the first Art School exhibition, took place at Rua Red Arts Centre in Tallaght, South County Dublin, in 2017. Thank you to artists John Beattie, Sarah Browne, Ella de Búrca, Priscila Fernandes, Mark O'Kelly, Maria McKinney and Sarah Pierce; the Fifth Year art students from Killinarden Community School who collaborated with Sarah Browne (Daiana Belciug, Courtney Boylan, Jamie Byrne, Jade Carkey, Brittany Daly, Rachel Deegan, Orla Dent, Leanne Gallagher, Katie Guerrine, Kelly Healy, Karl Jones, Reece Kinsella, Shane Lee, Meagan Nibbs, Megan O'Keefe, Chloe Russell, Nikki Sullivan and Chloe Tynan, and art teacher Sarah Edmondson); the Transition Year student painting collective from Our Lady's School who collaborated with Mark O'Kelly (Marie Bishop, Caoimhe Blaney Shorte, Shona Brady, Julie Bromwich, Emma Coffey, Katie Cowzer, Aisling Doyle, Saidhbh Duggan, Megan Giltrap, Miriam Hassan, Nicola Kelly, Rebecca Li, Aoife Lowe, Isabella Nash, Alexandra O'Reilly, Meriem Oukacine, Sinéad Richardson, Elaria Rossney, Marylou Ryan and Ellen Sweeney); the students and staff at Dublin 7 Educate Together National School; the Tallaght Community Arts performers who worked with Sarah Pierce on the live performance of *The Square* (Kelvin Akpaloo, Isobel Cummins, Cathal Dolan, Martha Knight, Adam Lynham-Clark, Charlie Webster and director Tony Fegan); Sven Anderson; artist Laura Smith for editing and cinematography; Dublin City Council public art manager Ruairí Ó Cuív for delivering a speech at the opening; writer Joanne Laws for writing the exhibition essay; and to director Maolíosa Boyle, Karen Phillips, Joyce Dunne, Lorna Kavanagh, Hugh McCarthy, Dave Reilly and all of the team at Rua Red.

The Art School residency *Birds of Prey* took place at St Mary's National School in Maynooth, County Kildare, in 2017. Thank you to artist Maria McKinney; the Fourth Class students at St Mary's; principal Peter Coakley; deputy principal Róisín Murphy; teachers Jacinta Gunn and Cathal Fenton; special needs assistants Angela Leavy and Peter Comiskey; the staff at the school; Maynooth University and the Froebel Department of Primary and Early Childhood Education; lecturers Brian Tubbart, Laura Thornton and Dr Triona Stokes; arts officer Lucina Russell; arts assistant Brenda Brady; and Kildare County Council Arts Office.

Art School moved into 2018 with *I Sing the Body Electric*, working with Scoil Ída Naofa, Mahoonagh National School and Ahalin National School in County Limerick in collaboration with EVA International. Thank you to artist Clare Breen and curators Maeve Mulrennan and Orlaith Treacy; the student curatorial teams; project assistants Stephen Murphy, Ciarán Nash and Mary Conroy; principals Yvonne Condron, Marie Geoghegan and Brid Liston; the teachers and school staff; Siobhan O'Reilly and Una McCarthy and Limerick City Gallery for making the collection available for the purpose of the project; director Matt Packer; administrative and operations manager Maria Casey; project photographer Deirdre Power; EVA International; and Creative Ireland.

Your Seedling Language, the first permanent artwork to evolve through Art School, was established at St Catherine's National School in Rush, County Dublin, and launched in 2019. Thanks to artist Adam Gibney, principal Ger Ó Sé and the students, teachers and staff at St Catherine's. This commission was funded by the Department of Education and Skills and the Per Cent for Art Scheme.

Working through these projects was only possible due to the kindness, generosity and support of my friends and family. I want to thank Sophie Von Maltzan for her remarkable endurance in the many, many conversations that we have had about Art School and *Curriculum* over these years, and for kindly and astutely pushing me to ask for help when I needed it. I am grateful to Sandra Atkins and Sarah Seigne and Anne Thompson for being sounding boards to help me remember how to communicate clearly about these projects. I want to thank Ann Keane for all of the walks, and her consistent confidence and assurance in my being able to complete this book. I want to thank my mother-in-law Sally Anderson for sharing all of her experience and ideas about education and pedagogy over the years. I also want to thank my mother, Kay Guy, for her support and humour along the way.

Finally and most importantly, I owe my deep gratitude to my daughter Molly Guy Lambton and my husband Sven Anderson, as the three of us have been together through every stage of this book and of Art School. All I have left is a word heap:

>endless love and support
>advice
>patience
>perspective
>camaraderie
>reflection
>conversations
>learning so much
>creativity
>
>Fighting!

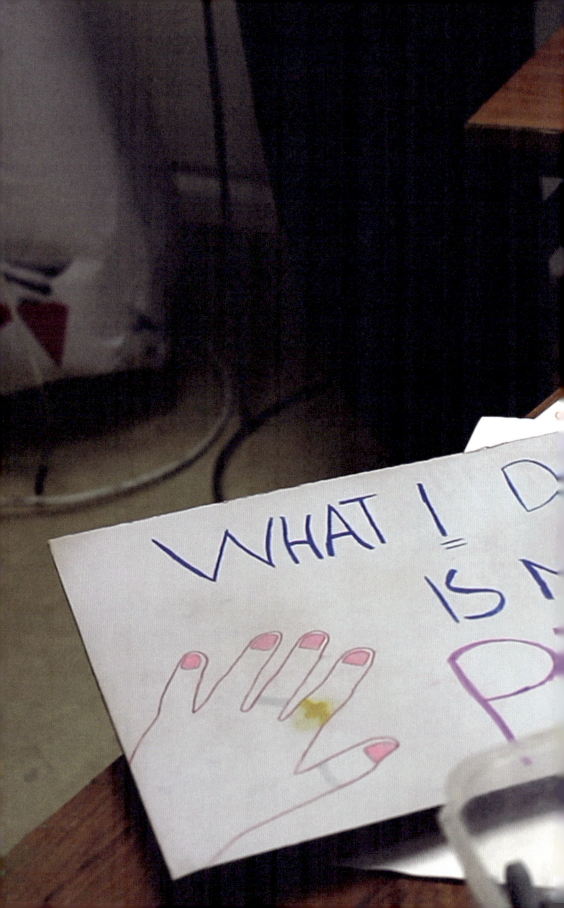

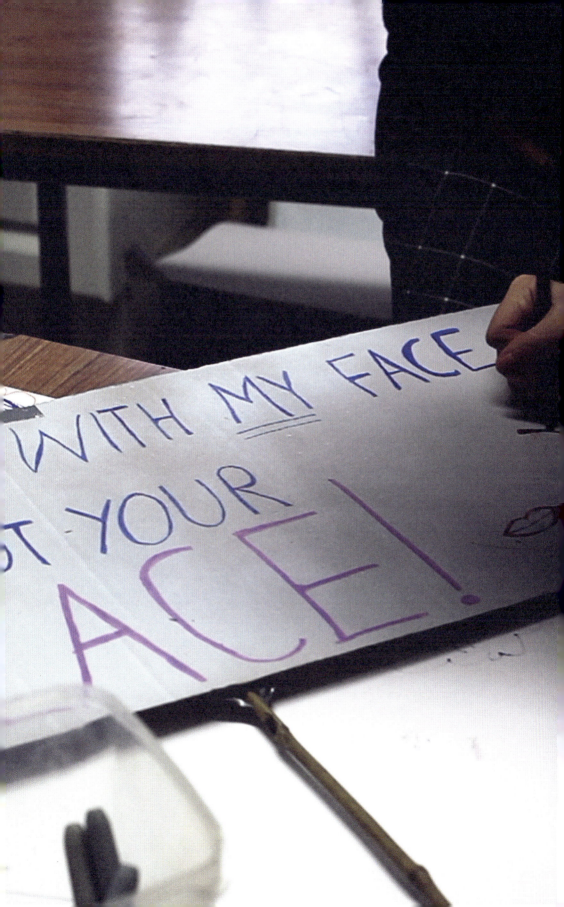

Contributors

Jennie Guy (Editor) is a curator, artist, writer and educator based in Dublin, Ireland. She holds a BA in English Literature and History from Trinity College, Dublin, and an MA in Visual Arts Practices from the Institute of Art, Design and Technology, Dun Laoghaire. Earlier in her career she worked in food and hospitality. She launched an independent artisanal food company and was instrumental in the introduction of Slow Food to Ireland. She is the founder and director of Art School, an experimental framework that explores strategies for placing artists within sites of education. In 2018, Guy developed *I Sing the Body Electric*, an education programme presented by EVA International. In 2016 she co-launched *Artists' Exercises*, an online platform for distributing artists' educational strategies featuring contributions from artists all over the world. Alongside her work with art and education, Guy curates and consults on public art commissions in Ireland. Recent commissions curated by Guy include Ruth Lyons' *Iontaise/Iontas* (2020), Adam Gibney's *Your Seedling Language* (2019) and David Beattie's *Reflectors* (2019). Guy presented the exhibitions *Field Recording* (2018) and *It's Very New School* (2017) as curator-in-residence at Rua Red Arts Centre. In conjunction with her independent practice, Guy manages the arts programme at Fire Station Artists' Studios in Dublin. Her writing has appeared in publications such as *Paper Visual Art*, *TransActions*, *Circa*, and *The Visual Artists' News Sheet*. Guy's artworks often manifest as portraits, including films, performances, installations and texts, such as *Before the Flood* (2015), *How to See Clearly from a Distance* (2014), *Reading Ensemble III* (2012), *Life is Beautiful* (2012), *Selected Crônicas* (2011) and *Melancholy Park* (2010).

Fiona Gannon (Assistant Editor) is an artist, writer and researcher living in Dublin. She graduated with a BA in Visual Arts Practice from the Institute of Art, Design and Technology in 2013, and soon afterwards took part in Workhouse Assembly, a collaborative and transdisciplinary project in Callan, Kilkenny, which explored the potential future use of a former workhouse with curators Rosie Lynch and Hollie Kearns (the project grew into Workhouse Union, visit at workhouseunion.com). She then worked as an intern on Studio Olafur Eliasson's Research and Communications team until autumn 2014 and completed her MA in Art and Research Collaboration from the Institute of Art, Design and Technology in 2016. Since graduating, she has written reviews for publications such as *Paper Visual Art*, *Art Monthly* and *Critical Bastards*, and has been focused on research around posthumanism and the infrastructuring of relationships. In 2017, she published a speculative book called *Into the Dark with the Light On* with arc public press about the human animal in relation to technology, and in 2018, she performed with collaborator Liliane Puthod a storytelling event called *I Sí* in the Phoenix Park after dusk at Samhain (when the Otherworld is nearest), exploring infrastructure and ghosts. From 2018 until 2019, she worked as an art teacher and as part of a Special Educational Needs (SEN) team in a secondary school, taking particular interest in the SEN care work needed even with 'Universal Design' incorporated into the class framework. She is currently researching boundaries, vulnerability and the ideology of transparency, through affective sculptural processes.

Neil Burkey (Copy-Editor) is a Dublin-based editor, author and occasional artist. He has worked on books for the Bush Theatre in London, the European Court of Human Rights in Strasbourg and the Hugh Lane Gallery in Dublin, and edited titles with topics ranging from electronic dance music, to the history of art, to Japanese keirin cycling. (Go to www.neilburkey.com for more.) His stories, articles and essays have been published in the *Dublin Review*, the *Irish Times* and the (UK) *Independent*.

Peter Maybury works as an artist, musician, graphic designer, and educator. His practice-based research encompasses design for print and screen, film, sound, artworks for exhibition, publishing, editing and curation. Peter has collaborated extensively with practitioners and institutions, editors and curators, in Ireland, Belgium, Luxembourg, UK, US, Italy and Canada. His work has been featured in key design publications including the seminal *Emigre* magazine. Music releases include several albums as Hard Sleeper and as part of the band Thread Pulls. His dual-screen film installation *Landfall* premièred momentarily at the *Where we live* festival in Dublin in March 2020. Peter lectures in Visual Communication at TU Dublin School of Creative Arts.

Clare Butcher is a curator and educator from Zimbabwe who cooks and collaborates as part of her practice. She is Curator of Public Programming and Learning for the Toronto Biennial of Art, before which she coordinated programmes such as *unsettling Rietveld Sandberg* in Amsterdam, the Netherlands, and *aneducation* for documenta 14 in Kassel, Germany. Clare has worked with museums, academies and communities in Europe and Southern Africa, and holds an MFA from the School of Missing Studies, an MA in Curating the Archive from the University of Cape Town and has participated in the De Appel Curatorial Program. Some collective and individual endeavours include *Men Are Easier to Manage Than Rivers* (2015); *The Principles of Packing...* on two travelling exhibitions (2012) and *If A Tree...* on the Second Johannesburg Biennale (2012).

Gerard Byrne is an artist based in Dublin. His work has been exhibited widely over the past twenty years. He was a Professor of Art at the Royal Danish Academy of Fine Art Copenhagen from 2007 to 2016. Since 2018 he has been Professor of Film at the Städelschule, Frankfurt.

Juan Canela lives and works in Barcelona as an independent curator and writer. He is artistic director of Zona Maco in Mexico City, co-founder of BAR project, Research and Symposium Associate of the osloBIENNALEN First Edition (2019–2024), a member of the Programs Committee at HANGAR, Barcelona, and part of the Present Future Curatorial Committee at Artissima, Turin. He has been Curator of the opening section at ARCO Madrid (2016–2017) and has curated projects at art institutions, galleries and independent spaces such as Palais de Tokyo, Paris; Centro Cultural de España Santo Domingo; Fundación Cerezales, León; CA2M, Madrid; Tiro al Blanco Gallery, Guadalajara; Tabakalera, San Sebastián; CRAC Alsace, Altkirch, France; SOMA Mexico, Mexico City; Fundació Miró, Barcelona; and La Ene, Buenos Aires. He was a member of the Guest Board for LIVE WORKS Performance Act Award at Centrale Fies, Milan (2018); he has attended the SYNAPSE Workshop 2015 at Haus der Kulturen der Welt, Berlin (2015); and was one of the speakers at Surrounding Education (2015) at De Appel Art Centre, Amsterdam. He has given lectures and workshops at FLORA ars+natura, Bogotá; Curando Caribe, República Dominicana; Bisagra, Lima; Instituto Torcuato Di Tella, Buenos Aires; and La Casa Encendida, Madrid. Upcoming projects include curating the Compositions programme at Gallery Weekend, Barcelona (2019), and acting as associate curator of Matadero Madrid Residencies Art Centre (2020). He frequently writes for magazines such as *A*Desk*, *Babelia El País*, *art-agenda*, *Terremoto* and *Mousse*.

Helen Carey is Director of Fire Station Artists' Studios, which provides substantial resources for the production of visual art, including living/working accommodation, large-scale sculptural work facilities, digital media production resources, and national and international curatorial development opportunities. She was previously Director of

Limerick City Gallery of Art and the inaugural Director of the Centre Culturel Irlandais, Paris. She is also an independent curator, with research interests covering subjects of historical significance such as state commemorations, and the social history of the nineteenth and twentieth centuries. Her most recent exhibitions include *The Souvenir Shop* (2016) by Rita Duffy, commemorating the Irish 1916 Rising, which was a national award and major Arts Council Open Call commission; *Crystalline* (2018) by Siobhan McDonald, an international touring exhibition examining changes over time in the climate and environment; and a Fire Station Artists' Studios exhibition, *EMBODIMENT* (2019), for Galerie Michaela Stock, Vienna, with Irish and Austrian performance artists. She has also completed public art commissions for public and private clients in both Ireland and the United Kingdom.

Daniela Cascella (Italy/UK) writes and researches forms of criticism that inhabit, echo and are haunted by their subjects: literature, voices and fictions of the self. Writing in English as a second language, writing as a stranger in a language, she is drawn towards unstable and uncomfortable forms of writing-as-sounding, and towards the transmissions and interferences of knowledge across cultures. She has written three books in English: *Singed. Muted Voice-Transmissions, After The Fire* (Equus Press, 2017), *F.M.R.L. Footnotes, Mirages, Refrains and Leftovers of Writing Sound* (Zer0 Books, 2015) and *En Abîme: Listening, Reading, Writing. An Archival Fiction* (Zer0 Books, 2012), and has published and lectured internationally. She teaches in the MA Sound Arts at LCC/University of the Arts London, was Assistant Professor in Writing in the Faculty of Art, Design and Music at the University of Bergen (2013–2018) and was a Research Fellow in the School of Arts at Oxford Brookes University (2013–2015).

Priscila Fernandes is a visual artist and co-Head of Department at BEAR (Base for Experiment, Art and Research) on the BA of Fine Arts of the ArtEZ Institute of the Arts, Arnhem, The Netherlands. Her practice is rooted in an ongoing research into education, play and the dialectics of work and leisure. She works in a broad range of media, including video, installation, sound, sculpture, drawing, painting, photography and text. She studied at the National College of Art and Design (BA Fine Art Painting) in Dublin and at the Piet Zwart Institute (MA Fine Art) in Rotterdam. She was a resident artist at Künstlerhaus Bethanien in Berlin, IAPSIS Stockholm and at the Irish Museum of Modern Art, Dublin. Her work has been exhibited widely. Recent exhibitions include *Live Uncertainty*—32nd São Paulo Biennial with the installation *Cuckoo Land and Other Futures*; *The Book of Aesthetic Education of the Modern School* at Foundation Joan Miró, Barcelona; *Back to the Sandbox: Art and Radical Pedagogy*, Reykjavik Art Museum; *Playgrounds*, Museum Reina Sofia, Madrid; *PIGS*, Artium Basque Museum; *Learning for Life*, Henie Onstad Kunstsenter, Oslo; *12 Contemporaries*, Serralves Museum, Porto; *Those bastards in caps come to have fun and relax by the seaside instead of continuing to work in the factory*, at TENT, Rotterdam; and *This is the Time. This is the Record of the Time* at Stedelijk Museum Bureau Amsterdam.

Andrew Hunt is a curator and writer based in London and Manchester and Professor of Fine Art and Curating at Manchester Metropolitan University. Since the early 2000s, he has worked on intimate solo exhibitions with significant international artists such as Mike Nelson, Elizabeth Price, Tris Vonna-Michell, Kai Althoff and Marc Camille Chaimowicz, as well as designers such as Fraser Muggeridge, Scott King, Jonathan Barnbrook, James Langdon, Åbäke, Manuel Raeder and Sara De Bondt on projects that range from minor printed ephemera to major publications, exhibition design and new branding for art institutions. From 2008 to 2014, he was Director of Focal Point Gallery (FPG) in Southend-on-Sea, where he developed the organisation into an international concern and oversaw its move into a new building (arch. Manalo & White, 2013). In 2012, he was a member of the Turner Prize jury. Between 2016 and 2017, he founded and directed the contemporary art festival Reading International and was a Research Fellow at Kingston University. He is currently working on a series of books titled *Interviews on Contemporary Painting*, which will contain conversations with forty international artists, writers, theorists and curators on the subject of new developments in the medium.

Alissa Kleist is a curator based in Belfast. In 2012, she co-founded Household, an organisation that initiates and delivers activities that engage with the past, present and future(s) of its localities and speculates about what public art is and can be, and how it can foster relationships and benefit people. As a co-director, she collectively runs the organisation, curating site-specific public programmes, exhibitions, student modules, residencies and events in community, non-institutional, public and neighbourhood spaces in Belfast. Kleist has held curatorial positions and worked as an independent curator at institutions in both Ireland and the UK. She is Project Curator (2018–2020) of the PS² Freelands Artist Programme, part of a UK-wide initiative to support and grow regional arts ecosystems by fostering long-term relationships and collaborations between emerging artists and arts organisations. As the Curator (Exhibitions) at the Centre for Contemporary Art (CCA) in Derry~Londonderry (2015–2018), she commissioned and delivered exhibitions and projects with emerging and established local and international artists. From 2011 to 2013, Kleist was one of the co-directors at Catalyst Arts, a collaborative, artist-led organisation with a polyvocal approach to the promotion of contemporary art practices. She regularly gives presentations at the invitation of cultural and educational institutions and critically writes about art for publications and online platforms.

Rowan Lear is an artist, writer and organiser, based in Glasgow. Her materials are old and new media, found images and objects, and language itself. She has contributed to publications and participated in exhibitions, talks, reading groups, residencies and symposia across the UK and further afield. In her practice, she tends to work collectively and in collusion with others, including non-human others. From 2017 to 2019, she co-organised a decolonial feminist study group called wrkwrkwrk; co-curated *Edge Effects*, a series of artist film screenings concerned with animality; and organised *Planetary Processing*, a peer forum and series of workshops at the Photographers' Gallery, London, for artists working with photomedia, ecology and embodiment. In 2017, she participated in the residency and exhibition *Rising from the Hill* at Cow House Studios, Wexford, and NCAD, Dublin, followed by a 2018 solo exhibition, *Adheres to the Tongue*, at the Muted Horn in Cleveland, Ohio. In 2019, she exhibited *Light Struck*, new work connecting photosensitivity and fermentation, at Lewisham Arthouse in London. She is currently a caretaker of Glasgow Seed Library, hosted by CCA Glasgow, and is plotting a hydrofeminist summer school for artists and thinkers on the wild, west coast of Scotland.

Annemarie Ní Churreáin is a poet and writer from the Gaeltacht region of north-west Donegal, Ireland. Her debut collection *Bloodroot* (Doire Press, 2017) was shortlisted for the Shine Strong Award in Ireland and for the Julie Suk Award in the USA. She is the author of a book of letterpress poems about Dublin entitled *Town* (The Salvage Press, 2018). Ní Churreáin has been awarded literary fellowships by Jack Kerouac House Florida, Hawthornden Castle in Scotland and Akademie Schloss Solitude in Germany. Her work has been published, toured and reviewed widely in Ireland and abroad. In 2016, she was the recipient of a Next Generation Artist Award by President Michael D. Higgins on behalf of the Arts Council. In 2018, Ní Churreáin was commissioned by Fire Station Artists' Studios to create *File Note II*. In 2019, she was Commissioned Writer at Temple Bar Gallery and Studios. Ní Churreáin is part of a poetry collaboration titled (S)worn State(s), which is a recipient of the inaugural Markievicz Award. Ní Churreáin is a 2019–20 Writer in Residence at Maynooth University, Kildare.

Nathan O'Donnell is a writer, researcher and one of the co-editors of the Irish journal of contemporary art criticism, *Paper Visual Art*. He has had work published in the *Dublin Review*, *gorse*, the *Irish Times*, the *Manchester Review*, *Apollo* and *3:AM*, among others. He is currently a Research Fellow at the Irish Museum of Modern Art. He has received bursary support from the Arts Council of Ireland as well as artists' commissions from IMMA, South Dublin County Council and Dublin City Council, and his first solo exhibition—focused upon student protest and ideas of discipline and indiscipline—took place at the Illuminations Gallery, Maynooth University, in March 2020. His first book, on Wyndham Lewis' art criticism, was published by Liverpool University Press in 2020, and he will edit the scholarly edition of the British avant-garde journal BLAST for the Oxford University Press' Critical Edition of Lewis' Collected Works. He lectures at Trinity College and on the MA Art in the Contemporary World at NCAD.

Sofía Olascoaga's practice focuses on the intersections of art and education: exploring encounters, think tanks and public programmes, and the involvement of artists, theorists, curators and educators with a wide range of institutional and independent interlocutors in experimental formats for collaborative work. Her ongoing research, *Between Utopia* and Disenchantment (*Entre utopía y desencanto*), critically assesses the collective memory and genealogies stemming from intentional community models developed in Mexico in recent decades, addressing ideas developed by Ivan Illich at the Centro Intercultural de Documentación (CIDOC) and their influential role in the practices of many Mexican and international thinkers. Olascoaga was Co-curator of the 32nd Bienal de São Paulo, *Incerteza Viva*, in 2016; Academic Curator at MUAC (Museo Universitario de Arte Contemporáneo—UNAM) in Mexico City (2014–2015); Research Curatorial Fellow at Independent Curators International, 2011; Helena Rubinstein Curatorial Fellow at the Whitney Museum of American Art's Independent Study Program, 2010; Workshop Clinics Director for the International Symposium of Contemporary Art Theory in Mexico City, 2012; and Head of Education and Public Programs at Museo de Arte Carrillo Gil in Mexico City 2007–2010. She received her BFA with honours from La Esmeralda National School of Fine Arts in Mexico City.

Matt Packer is a curator and writer living in Co. Clare, Ireland. He is currently Director/CEO of EVA International—Ireland's Biennial of Contemporary Art. Previous roles include Director, CCA Centre for Contemporary Art Derry~Londonderry (2014–2017); Associate Director, Treignac Projet (2013–2016); and Curator of Exhibitions and Projects, Lewis Glucksman Gallery (2008–2013). In an independent capacity he curated numerous exhibitions and projects, including *They Call Us the Screamers*, TULCA Festival of Visual Arts, Galway (2017) and *Disappearing Acts*, Lofoten International Art Festival, Norway (2015) (with Arne Skaug Olsen). He was part of the selection committee for the British representation at the Venice Biennale 2017 and one of the international mentors on the *What Could/Should Curating Do?* programme, Belgrade (2018/2019). He has written and published over 100 texts for artists' publications, magazines and journals including *Frieze*, *Kaleidoscope*, *Concreta*, *Source* and *Camera Austria*.

Helen Reed and Hannah Jickling have been collaborating since 2007 and are currently based in Vancouver, Canada, on the unceded territories of the Musqueam, Squamish and Tsleil-Waututh First Nations. Their projects take shape as public installations, social situations and events that circulate as photographs, videos, printed matter and artists' multiples. They are currently fascinated with the contact high intrinsic to collaborative research, especially in their recent projects with children. In autumn 2017, they released *Multiple Elementary*, a book that explores the elementary school classroom as a site for the invention and reception of contemporary art practices, published by YYZBOOKS. Their platform for research and production, *Big Rock Candy Mountain*, is ongoing in Vancouver and supported by Other Sights for Artists' Projects. Reed and Jickling are recipients of the 2016 Ian Wallace Award for Teaching Excellence (ECUAD), the 2017 Mayor's Arts Award for Emerging Public Art (City of Vancouver) and the 2018 VIVA Award (Shadbolt Foundation). In 2018, they were longlisted for the Sobey Art Award.

Sjoerd Westbroek is an artist living and working in Rotterdam, with a practice that involves drawing, teaching, studying and collaborating. He holds a BA in Fine Art in Education from ArtEZ Arnhem, a BA in Philosophy from Erasmus University Rotterdam and an MA in Fine Arts from Piet Zwart Institute, Rotterdam. Having exhibited both nationally and internationally, he was granted a research position at the Jan van Eyck Academy, a post-academic residency programme based in Maastricht, in 2013/2014. He often works with other artists, for instance as a founding member of artist initiative ADA, Area for Debate and Art; as a member of Barry (with Edward Clydesdale Thomson and Frans-Willem Korsten); and as a board member of Hotel Maria Kapel, Hoorn. Westbroek teaches at the Fine Art and Design Teacher Training programme of Willem de Kooning Academy and the Master Education in Arts programme at Piet Zwart Institute, Rotterdam.

divider images

p.12/13
Holding a position for a stop motion film during a residency at Blessington Community College with John Beattie (2014).

p.30/31
Screening a monochrome video on the classroom wall during a residency at Scoil Chonglais with John Beattie (2015).

p.98/99
Tracing marks on the gymnasium floor in a video made by students from Killinarden Community School in collaboration with Sarah Browne (2017).

p.210/211
Performers from Tallaght Community Arts performing *The Square*, a performance developed in collaboration with Sarah Pierce for the opening night of the exhibition It's Very New School at Rua Red Arts Centre (2017).

p.272/273
Running cables to an outdoor sound installation developed during a residency at Blessington Community college with Sven Anderson (2014).

p.286/287
Researching different forms of protest during a residency at Blessington Community College with Maria McKinney (2016).

p.288/289
Gathering residual materials at the end of a workshop at St. Paul's CBS—The Brunner—with Karl Burke (2017).

Bristol, UK / Chicago, USA